YOUR LIFE,
YOUR LEGACY

THE FUNDAMENTALS OF

EFFECTIVE ESTATE PLANNING

Cover design by: Dean Andrade

Prepared for printing by:

Laura Wilson
Wilson Advisors, LLC
Madison, Wisconsin 53719

Book printing by:

Publisher's ExpressPress
Ladysmith, Wisconsin 54848

Printed in the United States of America
by
Legacy Educational Publishing, LLC
7633 Ganser Way, Suite 100
Madison WI 53719

Special Edition, June 2009

Authors' Note

This book addresses important estate planning ideas for individuals and business owners. Although it is intended to provide a general introduction to the legal, accounting, tax, financial planning and investment issues that affect your estate plan, you should not rely upon this book as your sole source of information and advice for these important topics. Changes in the law, or in the interpretation of such laws, occur frequently and such changes made after this manuscript was completed may affect the recommendations made by the authors. Also, the recommendations made herein are general in nature and, therefore, may not be suitable for every reader.

A reference book like this one should never be seen as a substitute for professional assistance. Legal, accounting, tax, financial planning, investment or other advice should be obtained from a competent professional in that specific profession. We recommend that for your estate planning needs you consult with one of the Contributing Authors listed after the Introduction. These attorneys dedicate their legal practices to working with families to design and implement estate plans that meet each family's individual needs and desires. Your family's situation is unique and should receive individual attention.

IV

Contents

INTRODUCTION

This book is written to share with you the many benefits of Revocable Living Trust centered Estate Planning and to help you find a qualified attorney to help you design and mplement your estate plan. It is written by attorneys who believe that everyone has the right to do the following:

- Control their property during their lifetime
- Ensure that their property is available to take care of them and their loved ones in the event they become disabled
- Give what they have to whom they want, the way they want, and when they want;
- Wherever possible, save taxes, court costs, and professional fees.
  -

An estate planning pardigm shift is taking place in America today, and we are part of it. We have learned through our collective experiences that the old strategy of using a simple will to pass on property after death is no longer adequate. We believe that Estate Planning is an act of life and love, not an act of death and fear. We urge you to join in our quest to discover a new and better way of planning our estates.

All of the atttorneys who collaborated to create this work are committed to changing the way America plans.

CONTRIBUTING AUTHORS

John L. Becker
(262) 784-8277
205 Bishops Way
Suite 217
Brookfi eld, WI 53005

Sameer Chhabria
(847) 940-0607
300 Saunders Road
Riverwoods, IL 60015

Deborah B. Cole
(773) 643-4448
1525 E. 53rd Street
Suite 920
Chicago, IL 60615

Collin J. Dahl
(920) 854-7100
2350 Maple Drive #100
P.O. Box 259
Sister Bay, WI 54234

Irene Clarke David
(847) 382-6620
18-6 E. Dundee Rd.
Suite 112
Barrington, IL 60010

William A. Deitch
(630) 871-8778
600 West Roosevelt Road
Suite A-1
Wheaton, IL 60187

Joseph P. Earley
(715) 246-7555
539 South Knowles Avenue
New Richmond, WI 54017

Kenneth M. Fleck
(262) 376-2222
(877) 292-9557
7269 Highway 60
Cedarburg, WI 53012

Edward F. (Foss) Hooper
(800) 794-5548
(920) 993-0990
2 Systems Dr.
Appleton, WI 54914

Linda M. Jozefacki
(414) 964-1323
4321 N. Prospect Ave
Shorewood, WI 53211

Melburn E. Laundry
(847) 295-7177
410 Circle Lane
Lake Forest, IL 60045

Howard M. Lang
(847) 367-4460
700 Florsheim Drive
Suite 11
Libertyville, IL 60048-3757

Andrew C. (Drew) MacDonald
(920) 560-4646
4650 West Spencer Street
Appleton, WI 54914

Chris J. Mares
(920) 734-7000
2210 East Evergreen Drive
Appleton, WI 54913

Ketra A. Mytich
(309) 673-1805
6809 North Knoxville Avenue
Suite B
Peoria, IL 61614-2812

Teresa Nuccio
(847) 823-9576
1460 Renaissance Drive
Suite 105
Park Ridge, IL 60068

Steven H. Peck
(847) 940-0607
300 Saunders Road
Riverwoods, IL 60015

Mark D. Perkins
(630) 665-2300, ext 11
1751 S. Naperville Road
Suite 203
Wheaton, IL 60187

Chester M. Przybylo
(773) 631-2525
5339 N. Milwaukee Avenue
Chicago, IL 60630

Cliff J. Rice
(800) 303-7423
100 East Lincolnway
Valparaiso, IN 46383

Mark J. Rogers
(414) 289-9200
312 East Wisconsin
Suite 210
Milwaukee, WI 53202

Robert A. Ross
(920) 743-9117
55 South Third Avenue
PO Box 317
Sturgeon Bay, WI 54235-0317

David E. Shoub
(312) 827-2672
150 North Wacker Drive
Suite 2600
Chicago, IL 60606-1609

Mark T. Slate
(920) 398-2371
Central Wisconsin
33 North Bridge Street
P.O. Box 400
Markesan, WI 53946

William R. Slate
(920) 398-2371
Central Wisconsin
33 North Bridge Street
P.O. Box 400
Markesan, WI 53946

Ralph T. Stenger
(618) 277-5000
312 South Illinois
Belleville, IL 62220-2134

Gregory P. Turza
(847) 674-0200
7358 North Lincoln Avenue
Suite 150
Lincolnwood, IL 60712

Wayne W. Wilson
(608) 833-4001
7633 Ganser Way
Suite 100
Madison, WI 53719

Robert P. Wolfson
(630) 778-7778
1555 Naperville/Wheaton Road
Suite 101
Naperville, IL 60563

W. Ryan Zenk
(480) 969-5667
6900 E. Camelback Road #A39
Scottsdale, AZ 85251

CHAPTER ONE

PLAN NOW OR PAY LATER

BASIC CONCEPTS OF
ESTATE PLANNING

Estate planning, when done correctly, should above all else provide you with the peace of mind that comes from knowing you have done everything possible to protect yourself and your family. It does this by helping you achieve your hopes and accomplish your personal planning goals. Once these individual needs are addressed, good estate planning benefits your family by eliminating unnecessary probate costs, guardianship hearings, and death taxes.

What do you mean by "Estate Planning"?

The process of developing a sound estate plan of your own begins with understanding the basic ingredients common to all good estate plans. Our decades of experience working with thousands of clients have taught us that an estate plan is sound only if it helps accomplish several important goals. Almost universally, our clients state that they want their estate plans to achieve the following objectives:

- I want to control my property while I am alive;

- I want to take care of my loved ones and myself if I become disabled;

- I want to give what I have to whom I want, when I want, the way I want; and,

- Whenever possible, I want to save tax dollars, professional fees, and court costs.

If you have these same goals for yourself and your family, then this book is written specifically with you in mind because a good estate plan can help you accomplish each of these objectives. Without a good estate plan, you and your family will probably lose control over your property, suffer through unnecessary court proceedings, and pay unnecessay taxes and expenses. The lack of an estate plan may also deprive your family of many other legal protections otherwise available and also deprive them of the opportunity to receive from you a lasting legacy designed to bring your family closer together. Fortunately, all of these ills can be easily avoided by implementing a sound estate plan that passes your property to your loved ones in the way that you want.

All good estate planning starts with making sure that your property is legally owned in an appropriate way. The legal community uses the technical term "title" to describe how property is owned, and it is especially important that you understand the legal rules that govern title.

Why are the legal rules pertaining to title to important to planning my estate?

Title is important to designing an estate plan because you cannot plan for the disposition of property you do not own and control. Although you would think it easy for everyone to know what they do or do not own, the rules pertaining to property ownership are more complicated than they first appear. Unfortunately, families often unintentionally lose control and ownership of their property to others because these rules are widely misunderstood.

For example, many people who have written a will or a trust assume that all of their property will pass to their heirs according to the instructions in that document. That is not necessarily true! Of the thousands of estate plans we have reviewed for clients seeking our opinion, we have discovered that a great number of these plans will not work the way the clients think they will because the client's property has never been properly titled to ensure that it passes to whom they want, when they want, and how they want.

Regardless of what you may have heard or think, unless your property is correctly titled, even the best estate plan will fail to distribute it properly. Thus, in order for you to design an estate plan that accomplishes your goals, it is essential that you first understand the basic rules that govern the titling of property.

What are the different ways to title property?

Property can be titled in several different ways. The five most common ways of titling property are as follows:

- Fee simple;

- Tenancy in common;

- Joint tenancy;

- Tenancy in the entirety; and

- Community property.

Each of these ways of titling property differ from the others in three key ways:

- The amount of control the title owner possesses over the property while alive;

- The extent to which the owner is legally entitled to leave the property to others upon his or her death; and

- The extent to which creditors of the owner can make claims against the property.

Fee simple ownership exists when there is only one title owner. If you own property that is titled solely in your name you possess total legal control over it. This allows you to do with it whatever you want without anyone else's permission. You are free to retain, sell, or give the property away whenever desired. You also may say who will receive the property after your death. Finally, since only your individual legal rights are involved, any creditor of yours can make a claim against any of your fee simple property to satisfy a debt.

Tenancy in common ownership exists when two or more title owners hold the property together as *tenants in common.* If you own *tenancy in common* property, you share legal control of it with others. For example, if you and one other person own property as tenants in common, and you both own equal shares, you each own a fifty percent interest in it. If the property were sold, you would divide the profits equally.

However, ownership of tenancy in common property does not have to be in equal shares. Your share could be smaller or greater than another tenancy in common owner's share. The legal rule for tenancy in common property is that all co-owners share in the right to fully use and enjoy the property; therefore, even if you owned only a small fractional interest in *tenancy in common* property, you still have the right to use it whenever you want.

Although this arrangement is beneficial for those owning small shares, it can cause problems if two or more tenants in common desire to use the property at the same time or in different ways.

If you are a tenant in common, during your lifetime you can keep, sell, or gift your respective share of the property. Likewise, as a *tenant in common* you also may say who will receive the property after your death; however, creditor claims against a tenant in common can be made only against that tenant's share of the property.

Joint tenancy ownership is like tenancy in common in that two or more joint tenants own the property together and each owner has the right to enjoy its entire use. If you are a joint tenant, you have the right, while alive, to keep, sell, or gift your joint tenant's interest in the property to others.

Unlike a fee simple owner or a tenant in common, a joint tenant has no right to leave the joint tenant's interest to others *at death*. When one joint owner dies, by law that tenant's interest in the property is automatically extinguished and the surviving joint tenants continue to own the property together as joint tenants. Ultimately there will be only one final survivor when all of the other joint tenants have died. If you are the final surviving joint tenant, you will end up owning the entire property in *fee simple*. Creditor claims against a joint tenant can be made only against that tenant's share in the property.

As stated above, a joint tenant's interest is automatically extinguished upon that person's death. A benefit of this arrangement is that no probating of joint tenancy property ever occurs. The decedent's name is simply removed from the title and the others continue owning it together as joint tenants. While the probate free transfer of an asset is an attractive benefit of joint tenancy ownership, it often causes rather serious and unexpected consequences. Problems involving joint tenancy ownership include the following situations that frequently occur:

- Often family members purchase property together and title it as joint tenants without understanding that the last survivor will end up as the property's sole owner. Instead, they mistakenly think that if one of them dies that owner's share will pass to his or her spouse or children. Thus the family of the first joint tenant who dies is rudely surprised to learn they lose all rights to the property. If that were not bad enough, under the law the decedent joint tenant is treated as having made a gift of his or her interest in the property to the survivors. Thus the family of the decedent might have to pay gift taxes from the decedent's estate for property they never get.

- If a parent remarries and retitles the family home in joint tenancy with the new spouse, the children of the first marriage will lose all rights to the home if the parent dies before the new spouse.

- If an elderly parent puts the family home in joint tenancy with an adult child, the parent loses exclusive control over the home. The parent will not be able to refinance or sell the home without the child's approval. Also, the parent's home becomes exposed to the child's liabilities including automobile accidents, debts, bankruptcies, and claims of the child's spouse if there is a divorce. If there is more than one child named as joint tenant, all of these dangers are multiplied.

- If an elderly parent retitles savings or investment accounts in joint tenancy with one child, expecting that child to share it with siblings after the parent passes on, there can be unintended gift tax consequences, even assuming the child shares it with the others (which does not always happen).

- If a child named as a joint tenant dies first, the property will be taxed first in the child's estate and then probated and taxed a second time in the parent's estate.

Tenancy by the entirety ownership is a way married couples in some separate property states, can title their primary residence to provide creditor protection for a surviving spouse. Following the death of the first spouse, the home titled as tenancy by the entirety automatically passes to the surviving spouse free of probate. Creditors of *both* spouses (such as a mortgage company or credit card company) may take this property, but creditors of only *one* spouse cannot. This form of ownership may be a good choice of title if either spouse might someday be subject to business or professional liability since the property is protected from creditor claims.

A major concern arises with property titled in tenancy by the entirety if there are children from a prior marriage of either spouse. When one spouse dies the surviving spouse will inherit the home while the children of the deceased spouse will be disinherited.

Community Property ownership is a way married couples in community property states can title their property to reflect that they each own half of the property. In some states community property is also referred to as "Marital Property." Owning property as community property can help couples escape unnecessary capital gains taxes. Upon the death of one spouse the entire amount of community property gets a step-up in cost basis. This means the surviving spouse can sell property without having to pay capital gains tax after the death of his or her spouse. Community property tax treatment is available in only a limited number of states.

What happens if I do not plan my estate?

If you do not plan your estate, you will leave what is legally known as an "intestate estate", one in which the deceased has left no instructions. The families of those who fail to plan their estates have a rude surprise awaiting for them - the government will fill in the blanks with its own plan. After debts, probate costs, and taxes are paid, the courts will divide the estate according to the laws of intestate succession.

*If you do not plan your estate,*you may not know who your beneficiaries are. Some states provide that the estate of a married decedent goes entriely to the surviving spouse, provided there are no children from another marriage. Other states provide that the surviving spouse receives only half of the decedent's estate with the other half going to any children or their decedents. The first example may result in the children being disinherited, especially if the surviving spouse remarries, while the second example may leave the surviving spouse with inadequate resources to maintain an adequate lifestyle.

If you do not plan your estate and a minor child is entitled to receive an inheritance by law, the court will place the inheritance into a custodial trust. No withdrawals can be made without first obtaining the permission of the court. Whatever is left of your child's inheritance will be given to your child on his or her eighteenth birthday - with no guidance whatsover. Since few eighteen year olds have the maturity to properly handle a windfall inheritance, it is likely the inheritance will be totally wasted in a short period of time.

If you do not plan your estate and you have no spouse or children, most states provide that distributions will be made to your parents. If your parents are in a nursing home or receiving government assistance, who do you think gets the inheritance?

If you do not plan your estate and fail to appoint the personal representative (executor) you want to administer it, the court will appoint a personal representative of its own choice for you. Children or other heirs may have equal legal rights to be named the estate's personal representative which may lead to fights over whom should be named. This often leads to family feuds and court battles that could have been avoided had the parents simply named their own personal representatives.

If you do not plan your estate, the personal representative may be forced to pay for an expensive bond to insure the estate. This is money that could otherwise have gone to your loved ones.

If you do not plan your estate and you and your spouse both die prematurely, the probate court will appoint the guardian it chooses for your minor children instead of the ones you could have, but failed, to name yourselves. In other words, a stranger to the family will get to decide who tucks in your children at night and takes care of all of their other needs.

If you do not plan your estate, the courts will maintain continuing jurisdiction over any inheritance left for your children. Court permission is needed to use the inheritance and the court is likely to require an annual accounting of every penny spent. The result is that additional accounting and attorney's fees must be paid out of the inheritance every year until your child becomes eighteen.

How can I prevent having an intestate estate?

You can prevent having an intestate estate by leaving written instructions of your own. One way of leaving such instructions is by writing a will.

What is a will?

A will is a written document that tells the court how to divide your property at the time of your death. It also tells the court who should be the guardian for your minor children and your personal representative. Wills are filed with the court at time of death, and the court oversees the administration of the will through a process known as probate.

What is probate?

Probate is a legal court proceeding, supervised by a probate court judge, that is used to gather a deceased person's assets, pay creditors, court costs, and taxes and then distribute what is left to those entitled to receive it. In probate proceedings, the court sets the time limit in which creditors may file claims. The probate estate cannot be closed until the period for filing claims has expired and settlement with each creditor has been resolved. In general, you can expect a probate proceeding to last one year or longer. There have been many notable cases that have been tied up in probate court for several years.

The probate process allows creditors to make claims for debts incurred during the deceased's lifetime and allows the estate to pursue other legal actions pertaining to the decedent. Notice of the probate proceeding must be given to all known creditors and to all creditors who might be known after careful investigation. It must also be given to all relatives who may be legal heirs, even if they are not included in the will.

Are there any advantages of probate?

Advocates of probate argue that because probate proceedings are held in open court, it benefits potential heirs by providing everyone equal access to information contained in the probate record. They also argue that court supervision of the probate process benefits society by providing an orderly way of wrapping up a decedent's estate. They further argue that additional benefits exist in that institutions dealing with probate court orders recognize them as binding, that rights of lost heirs are severed, that claims not timely filed can be legally barred, and that the estate may pursue any litigation deemed necessary.

What are the disadvantages of probate?

The disadvantages of probating a will are many. The probate process is expensive, time consuming, and intrusive. Court costs, attorney fees, personal representative fees, bonds, and accounting fees all add up. The cost of probate is often between 3% and 8% of the gross value of an estate (up to eight thousand dollars for a hundred thousand dollar estate). If your estate is probated without a will, the costs of probate may be even greater.

The probate process is a notoriously protracted legal procedure. Studies in one state reveal that the median time for settlement is thirteen months. If the probate proceedings are contested, the ensuing legal battle can take several years.

Probate proceedings also intrude on a family's privacy. Probate proceedings take place in open court where the family's private financial records are made a public record. The family is forced to reveal for public inspection a listing of all of the family's savings, investments, and real estate. Also, now that many probate courts are making their records available on-line, anyone with a computer can easily access your family's probate records. In some cases, this easy access has led to identity-theft.

The estate is vulnerable to attack during probate proceedings from unhappy relatives and to suits from creditors who must receive certain legal notices. It is not unheard of for someone to file a claim in a probate proceeding simply as a way of forcing the estate to settle the claim in order to avoid an expensive legal fight.

Can probate be avoided?

Yes, fortunately probate can be avoided. As already discussed, probate proceedings can be avoided by titling property with someone else in joint tenancy. Such property will be transferred to the surviving joint tenant probate free. Because joint tenancy property passes probate free, many individuals mistakenly believe they do not need further planning if everything is titled in joint tenancy. But as discussed above, joint tenancy can result in property passing to unintended heirs, risks unforeseen tax consequences, and can result in loss of assets to lawsuits and other misfortunes.

Furthermore, an estate plan that relies only on joint tenancy ownership fails to provide any protection if one or both joint tenants become disabled by illness or accident. For example, if a husband and wife own property as joint tenants and the husband suffers a stroke, it may be legally difficult or impossible for the wife to make the decisions necessary to handle the couple's property without petitioning the court to be appointed the legal guardian of the disabled husband. This is a major pitfall of joint tenancy ownership that many couples unfortunately fail to anticipate.

In some community property states, probate can also be avoided for married couples who title their property as community property so that it passes probate free to the surviving spouse. Again, this provides no protection if one or both spouses become disabled and does not provide a mechanism to transfer assets to the next generation at the death of the second spouse.

Is there a better way to avoid probate?

Yes! A simple and superior way of avoiding probate is to place your property in a trust so that it passes probate free. To learn more about trusts, turn to the next chapter.

CHAPTER TWO

ESTATE PLANNING WITH TRUSTS

As discussed in Chapter One, there are serious consequences awaiting you and your family if you fail to properly plan your estate. The dangers of owning property in joint tenancy were discussed as well as the government's default plan, which will control your estate if you become disabled or die. To determine whether the government's default plan is the option you want for yourself and your family, simply ask yourself the following questions:

- Will the government's default plan keep my family out of guardianship court if I become disabled?

- Will the government's default plan keep my family out of probate?

- Will the government's default plan protect my family's privacy?

- Will the government's default plan create the least dela and hindrance for my family?

- Will the government's default plan make sure that my family pays the least amount of court costs and legal fees?

- Will the government's default plan make sure that my family pays the least amount of taxes?

As the answer to each of the above questions is an emphatic, "NO!", you will want to protect yourself and your family by proactively planning your estate. In our experience, trusts are the best legal tools available to plan your estate.

What is a trust?

A trust is a written legal document that provides instructions on how the property titled in the trust's name is to be managed. These written instructions can provide important legal benefits.

There are generally three people who are involved with trusts. First is the person who *makes* the trust. This person is therefore appropriately known as the "Trustmaker" or as is the case with married couples planning together in one trust, "Joint Trustmakers". Second is the person or institution (like a bank) *entrusted* by the Trustmaker to carry out the trust's instructions. This person is known as the "Trustee." Third is the person who *benefits* from the trust. This person is known as the "Trust Beneficiary."

One advantage of Revocable Living Trusts is that the same person who makes the trust can also be, and usually is, the Trustee and the Beneficiary of his or her own trust. Therefore you can make a trust, be the Trustee who manages it, and also be the one who benefits from it.

Trusts have been used since the Middle Ages and actually predate wills. They can also take various forms. Two main types of trusts are "Testamentary Trusts" and "Living Trusts."

What is a Testamentary Trust?

When a person drafts a will, sometimes they do not want the inheritance to go immediately upon their death to a spouse or child. Instead, they want the property to be managed for the beneficiary's protection over an extended period of time. One way to accomplish this is to state in the will that upon the maker's death, a Testamentary Trust will be created to manage the inheritance for the beneficiary. A Testamentary Trust, like a will, is legally effective only after you die and cannot provide any estate planning protections to you or your family during your lifetime.

Testamentary trusts are created in wills and like wills they are court supervised as part of the required probate court proceedings. This supervision continues until the probate is ended. This means that if you create a testamentary trust to manage assets for your children until they turns thirty years old, your family will have to deal with probate court proceedings year after year until your youngest child turns thirty. The best estate planning attorneys seldom use testamentary trusts because of this negative consequence. Instead, "Living Trusts" are the legal tool of choice used to meet the estate planning needs of most people.

What is a Living Trust?

Living Trusts are a special type of trust that go into legal effect immediately upon their signing, i.e., when the Trustmaker is still alive. They are also known as *"inter vivos"* trusts, which means "during life" in Latin. This distinguishes them from testamentary trusts, which, as discussed above, become legally effective only after the Trustmaker dies. Living Trusts therefore offer lifetime planning opportunities (such as instructions on how to manage your property if you become disabled) that simply cannot be had with a testamentary trust which take effect when it is too late.

Living Trusts are increasingly being used as the ideal solution for those who no longer want to expose themselves to the dangers of joint tenancy or force the estate to go through probate with a will. There are so many advantages to using trusts that recent studies report that up to half of all people who now plan their estates are using trusts instead of wills.

We are not surprised by this trend. The advantages of a properly designed and funded Living Trust include the ability to plan for a possible disability, legitimate tax avoidance, asset protection for the surviving spouse, individualized planning to protect your spouse and children, enhanced privacy, and probate avoidance. Also, because a properly drafted Living Trust can own any type of stock and participate in partnerships and limited liability companies, they can be used to smoothly transfer the family business to the next generation. If you own a small business, a Living Trust can enhance your business succession planning.

Furthermore, with a Living Trust one can still take advantage of the probate process if desired. The difference is that with a Living Trust the family has the choice of deciding whether probate court proceedings have any benefit – it is not forced into probate as happens to those who fail to plan or plan with simple wills.

Living trusts also come in several different types. The most commonly used living trust is the *"Revocable* Living Trust*"*.

What is a Revocable Living Trust?

The term, "revocable," means that the instructions of these trusts can be amended whenever the Trustmaker desires. These trusts are popular because they provide the Trustmaker the maximum flexibility in controlling the trust assets and the ability to change the plan whenever desired. While parents are alive and healthy, they act as the trust's Trustee and have total control over the property in it; however, if one or both parents suffer a disability, the trust's detailed instructions state how the parents should be cared for and how property held in the trust should be managed. Additional instructions state how the children and other loved ones should be cared for after the parents die. Since these trusts are "revocable," their instructions can be changed or canceled at any time so long as the Trustmaker is still legally competent. Also, property can be place into or removed from the trust anytime the Trustmaker desires.

How does one place property into a Revocable Living Trust?

If you create a trust, you will need to decide what property should be placed into your trust so that your Trustee gains legal control over it. Property is placed into a trust simply by changing its title to name the trust as its legal owner. This process of changing title is called "funding" the trust.

Almost any type of property can be funded into a trust. The funding process consists of simply signing documents that name the trust as the new owner of your property. For example, some assets such as real estate, are funded into a trust by preparing and signing a new deed that names the trust as the new owner.

Other assets such as savings accounts, are funded into a trust by signing a new signature card that names the trust as the new owner of the account. Still other assets (personal property including household furnishings, jewelry, etc.), are funded into a trust by signing a document known as an "assignment" that names the trust as its new owner.

What are the benefits of funding a Revocable Living Trust?

Funding a trust takes some work, but it is well worth the effort for one very important reason: the Trustee has legal control only over property titled in the trust's name. Any property not titled in the name of the trust is never legally owned by it, and property not owned by the trust is in danger of having to be probated when its owner dies; however, property that is properly titled in the name of the trust never has to go through probate court because trusts never die!

If the funding process sounds confusing to you, thinking of it in another way might help. Some have described a Revocable Living Trust as a "magic box" in which you place ownership of your property. You just open the top of the box and place into it the title to the house, the car, the checking account, the investment account, and anything else desired. Since you can name yourself as the Trustee of your own trust, you will maintain legal control over everything you put into your magic box. At any time you want, you can just reach into the box and take out the title to any asset and do with it as you please. You can sell, trade, invest, or give away any trust asset just as if you never had a trust. And at your death, it is as if the magic box is automatically handed to your designated successor trustee to administer your property according to your instructions. All this happens without your property being probated.

What instructions can a Revocable Living Trust contain?

The instructions contained in a Revocable Living Trust are limited only by the imagination and creativity of the Trustmaker. Nonetheless, most trusts will contain several important instructions including who will serve as Successor Trustee, what happens if a Trustmaker becomes disabled, and who will benefit from the trust after the Trustmaker dies.

What successor trustee instructions should be included in the trust?

Some of the most important instructions in Revocable Living Trusts pertain to who will replace the Trustmaker if the Trustmaker can no longer serve as a Trustee because of disability or death. The Successor Trustee will assume the legal responsibility of managing the trust's assets according to its instructions. Accordingly, the Successor Trustee must be exceptionally trustworthy, excel at managing property of considerable value, and be capable of following detailed legal instructions. A detailed discussion of a Trustee's responsibilities is presented in the chapters that follow.

What disability instructions should be included in the trust?

It is impossible for you to plan for a potential disability in a will, but Revocable Living Trusts are ideal legal tools for this vital planning need. On any given day, a person has a seven times greater chance of becoming disabled than of dying. Therefore, planning for the possibility of a disability is only common sense. As planners, we believe that a Revocable Living Trust is not complete unless it contains specific instructions for the Trustee to follow if the Trustmaker becomes disabled.

For example, many of our clients tell us that if they become disabled they want to be cared for in their homes as long as medically feasible. In such instances, the trust can contain individualized disability instructions such as the following:

• Authority to use trust assets to maintain the home so

long as it is occupied and to retrofit it for handicapped accessibility if necessary;

- Authority to pay for services such as visiting nurses, twenty-four hour care, hospice, and other needed care-givers to make staying at home a reality; and

- A statement of the desire to participate in normal activi-ties of daily life to the maximum extent possible includ-ing outings, recreation, travel, and religious or spiritual involvement.

What instructions pertaining to the trust's beneficiaries should be included?

Detailed instructions can be included in your trust that will enable you to leave what you want, to whom you want, when you want, and in the way you want just as if you were still alive and personally giving those instructions. You can be as creative as you desire and specify the conditions and timing of distributions to your loved ones. For example, if your children are minors, you can leave detailed instructions that inform the Trustee how to use trust assets to raise your children and the preferred type of schooling to provide for them.

Alternately, your living trust can be drafted to benefit any number of people in exactly the way you want. Possibilities in-clude friends, grandchildren, or even charities. Such planning can be designed to benefit them immediately or even over a period of several generations.

Are there any other benefits of having a Revocable Living Trust?

There are several other benefits of having a Revocable Living Trust. These include the following:

- Revocable Living Trusts are private documents that do not require court approval. Your beneficiaries will not have to wait for court permission to approve distributions of trust property. Outsiders and potential predators will also be prevented from learning the terms of your estate plan and using the knowledge against your loved ones.

- Court challenges to wills are successful 25% of the time. A Living Trust is more difficult to attack partly because its instructions are not readily available to relatives or others who might not be happy with these instructions.

- A Living Trust can hold property owned by a family in more than one state and save the family the cost and difficulty of conducting probates in multiple states.

For all these reasons and many others, Revocable Living Trusts are the legal tools that we find most often best accomplish our client's planning goals.

What else about Revocable Living Trusts is important to know?

There are three common misconceptions about Revocable Living Trusts. The first is a mistaken belief by some that putting your property in a Revocable Living Trust will protect it from creditors. This is simply not true. If you retain the legal right to use the property in your trust however you please, your creditors can go after it. While there do exist some types of trusts that provide some creditor protection for the beneficiary, Revocable Living Trusts do not fall into that category.

A second misconception is that placing property into a Revocable Living Trust will protect it from nursing home costs. The assets in a revocable trust remain "countable" for Medicaid purposes so they do not protect your assets from being used for nursing home care.

A third misconception about Revocable Living Trusts is that they can be used to avoid income taxes. Again, this is not true. Placing your property in a Revocable Living Trust will not change your personal income tax status or obtain for you any favorable income tax advantages. For income tax purposes, the IRS will continue to treat the property as if you still individually own it. Similarly, a Revocable Living Trust does not increase any income tax burden.

Unscrupulous individuals sometimes promote these misconceptions about living trusts in an attempt to sell trust forms or other services and make a quick profit. Do not believe them.

Revocable Living Trusts are excellent tools for avoiding costly guardianship hearings, probate proceedings, and legal fees and costs. Drafted correctly, they can help your family legitimately avoid estate taxes and keep you in control of your property to benefit you and your loved ones. In order to obtain these benefits, you need and deserve the quality legal advice available only from a qualified estate planning attorney.

Family Trust - Credit Shelter -
Beneficiary:
Trustee:

CHAPTER THREE

TINY TREASURES DEMAND BIG PLANNING MEASURES

Planning to protect our families in the event of our disability or death is not an easy thing to do. Aside from the necessity of facing one's own mortality, there are often emotionally charged issues that must be faced when we plan for our children.

Throughout our lives we make many plans, usually for happy occasions like birthdays, education, vacations, weddings, and retirement, but when it comes to designing a sound estate plan that protects our families, necessary planning is often neglected if not actively avoided.

The sad fact is that most parents provide better instructions to a baby-sitter who looks after their children for a few hours than they leave for the care of their children in the event of their own permanent disability or death.

What happens if parents fail to plan for their children?

If you fail to leave instructions for how your children are to be taken care of in the event of your death, some stranger in a probate court will make those decisions for you. No one knows or loves your children more than you. No one knows better than you their individual needs and how to best protect them. Why would you leave such important decisions to strangers?

What issues are involved in planning for minors?

When planning for minors, typically our clients ask us four major questions:

- How can I best make gifts to minor children during my lifetime?

- Who should be named my child's guardian if I suffer an untimely death?

- How should I leave property to my children if they are still minors when I die?

- How can I plan for a child who is disabled or has other special needs?

Planning in this area involves far more than mere economics. It involves creating an environment that will allow minor children to experience both loving care and economic security as they grow into adulthood. This planning should begin while you are still alive. One estate planning opportunity you have is your ability to make lifetime gifts to your children.

What issues are involved in making lifetime gifts to children or grandchildren?

When planning their estates, many parents and grandparents want to learn the best way they can make lifetime gifts to children or grandchildren. These gifts are usually intended to build a college fund for the child while also reducing the donor's taxable estate. Although these parents and grandparents are to be commended for their proactive approach to protecting their loved ones, there are several pitfalls for the unwary in such lifetime planning.

Financial professionals often advise parents to establish custodial accounts for minors under the Uniform Transfer to Minors Act (UTMA). These accounts are easy to recommend because they are easy to establish and require few formal documents. The problem with this recommendation is that the child will be given all of the account assets when he or she turns twenty-one.

There is nothing magical about reaching one's twenty-first birthday. Not all children are financially mature at that age and many need further guidance. If there are substantial sums in the account, the biggest question many children often face is, "What color should the Porsche be?" Some of the best parents in the world have raised children who cannot handle money. This lack of control is a major drawback that makes an UTMA definitely not the right vehicle for the parent or grandparent who desires to guide the child's use of the assets.

If you want to retain control over how and when distributions are made from a child's account, a Minor's Demand Trust is an excellent option that should be explored. With a Minor's Demand Trust, the parent or grandparent retains control over how the trust assets can be used while still escaping gift taxes that would otherwise be due. To accomplish this two requirements must be met. First, annual gifts are made that are kept under the annual gift tax exemption. Second, each time a gift is made the minor is given the legal right to demand the gift during a specified period of time (a window of opportunity). This withdrawal right poses no particular problem because, since the child is still a minor when the gift is made, it is of course the parent who decides whether to exercise the child's withdrawal right. The parent can simply waive the demand right and instead invest the funds for the child's future needs.

Another benefit of a Minor's Demand Trust is that distributions are not limited to educational needs. The Trustee can use trust assets for the benefit of the child as desired or deemed appropriate.

Who should be named the guardian for minor children?

Perhaps no issue is more difficult for parents to address than who will take care of the children if the parents are unable to care for the children themselves. This question is so important that we have devoted the entire next chapter to it.

What issues are involved in leaving assets to minors upon your death?

Once you decide how to best make lifetime gifts to provide for a child's future educational needs and financial security, and determine who will be the child's guardian, the next step is to protect the inheritance. A "simple will," suggested by some attorneys, is not an adequate tool for this important task.

Such "simple wills" can subject your children to unnecessary and intrusive court proceedings, excessive costs, lost privacy and extended delays. Moreover, with ongoing court proceedings, every trip to the attorney's office or courthouse reminds the children of their loss. Instead of accepting such questionable advice, consider consulting an experienced estate planning attorney who can efficiently and creatively set up a Living Trust that incorporates your most cherished values, hopes, wishes, dreams and aspirations for your minor children.

A major planning difficulty we often see stems from the desire of many parents to treat all of their children equally. As a result of this desire, it is not uncommon for parents to divide their estates into equal separate shares for each child. While this simplistic approach sounds equitable, it can lead to drastically unfair results. What is fair is not always what is equal. The truth of this is seen in how most of us raise our children.

When asked, most parents admit that they do not use a ledger to keep track of money spent on each child. For example, if one child displays musical talent most parents would not hesitate to invest in piano lessons and even buy a piano if the family can afford it. Having made such a large investment for one child, they do not immediately give an equal amount to the other less talented children.

The problem with taking an automatic "equal division" approach in planning your estate is that it imposes a rigid one-size-fits-all plan on the children regardless of their age, economic circumstances, or their individual needs, strengths and weaknesses. Of course we all love our children equally but we should never fail to plan for them as individuals.

In our experience, the use of a "Common Trust" for minor children more closely mirrors the flexibility that parents use in raising their children. A Common Trust comes into effect upon the deaths of both parents. The alternatives in design are almost endless, but the cornerstone of every Common Trust is to provide for all your children's needs from a common source just as if you were still alive. Authors and preeminent estate planning attorneys, Robert A. Esperti and Renno L. Peterson, have aptly nicknamed this kind of trust a "soup-pot trust" and describe it as follows:

> "Can you recall your mom's soup specialty? If it was like our moms', it had just about everything in the pantry and refrigerator in it. When it was ladled out, the hungrier children at the table got more than those who weren't as hungry. Some got more meat, because it was their favorite; some got more vegetables or rice or noodles. If a particular brother or sister had a penchant for a particular ingredient, that ingredient was always

found in abundance in his or her bowl. Mom controlled and monitored the whole process to make sure that everyone was nourished and as happy as possible, and she ultimately decided who got what." (Esperti and Peterson, *Loving Trust,* Viking Penguin, 1994).

In an estate plan that incorporates a Common Trust, the Trustee serves as the "mom" in the soup story told above. The Trustee decides who gets what based upon the individual present and anticipated needs and desires of the children and the available trust assets. Since the Trustee's job is to follow the Trust's instructions, it is a good idea that those who desire to incorporate a Common Trust into their estate plan give their Trustee guidance as to the specific needs of each child.

While it is a good idea to place assets in a Common Trust while the children are young, at some point the trust will have fulfilled its purpose, and it becomes time to distribute whatever remains to the now older, and hopefully mature, children. The question then becomes, "What is the right time to end the Common Trust?" While this is an individual decision based on the family situation, most common trusts contain instructions that state that the Trustee should keep funds in the Common Trust until the youngest child reaches a certain age or finishes college. If the Common Trust were ended and the assets distributed when the oldest child reaches a certain age or finishes college, the youngest child could be deprived of the opportunity to receive Trust assets for education or other needs. It is much more equitable to keep the Common Trust intact until the youngest child receives the same level of care that was given to older siblings.

To alleviate the danger that the older children may feel that they are being punished by having their inheritance delayed until a much younger sibling grows up, trust instructions can be included that allow the Trustee to advance money or property to an older child for extraordinary needs or opportunities. This "advancement" is then taken out of that child's share when the Common Trust is terminated and the assets distributed among the children.

Another good idea to use in planning for your children is to build incentives into the Trust to motivate the child to live responsibly and develop good work habits. For example, incentives can be drafted that reward the children for maintaining a good grade point average, graduating from college, that assist with a down payment on a home, or match earned income among many other possible incentives. The possibilities for designing incentives that are individually tailored for the needs of your children are limitless.

When the time comes for the Common Trust to be divided, there are two main options. One can decide that all of the trust assets should be immediately divided and distributed outright to the children to do with as they please. This option is appropriate if the children are all older, leading successful lives, and the parent does not feel the need to protect the inheritance for a variety of reasons. Alternately, instead of just surrendering total control of the inheritance to the children, the parent can decide to keep each child's inheritance in a protective trust established specifically for that child. These protective trusts contain instructions for the management and distribution of trust assets tailored to the individual needs of a specific child. Again, the possibilities and alternatives for designing these trusts are endless.

Property can be kept in trust for a beneficiary's entire lifetime. In this situation a Trustee is appointed to decide when and how much of the trust assets to distribute. This type of planning makes sense not only if a child has spendthrift tendencies or a drug or alcohol problem, but the trust can also provide protection for your child from a failed marriage or claims of creditors.

If you have a child who will never be able to handle money, keeping that child's inheritance in the trust with instructions to the Trustee to provide for his or her health, education, maintenance, and support would be a wise and loving choice. Alternately, a parent can decide to space trust distributions over several years. This prevents children from misspending the entire inheritance all at once by giving them time to mature. The last thing a parent wants is to destroy a child with an inheritance.

If your child has reached maturity and is fiscally responsible, the trust instructions can be quite flexible and allow withdrawal of trust funds whenever he or she wants. Often the child becomes the Trustee of his or her own trust. Although the child has access to the funds, if properly drafted, the Trust will protect the inheritance from creditor claims, lawsuits, and divorcing spouses. In our litigious and divorce-prone society, such protections are becoming increasingly necessary.

Unfortunately, in some families a child may never be able to provide for himself or herself due to a physical or mental disability or some other special need. In these cases special planning is needed for the special child.

How can I plan for a child who is disabled or has other special needs?

The most effective way to make sure a child with special needs is properly provided for upon your death is to create a Special Needs Trust for the child's benefit. A Special Needs Trust is administered by a Trustee whose duty is to provide for the financial and medical needs of the special child in accordance with the written instructions in the trust. A Special Needs Trust will protect the assets you leave for the use of the child from the unscrupulous. The child may also need a guardian who will oversee the child's emotional, religious, and social needs.

Are there any problems with creating a Special Needs Trust?

A Special Needs Trust can be drafted to meet the needs of the individual child. The instructions in the Special Needs Trust should also be designed so that the child does not become ineligible to receive federal or state benefits to which the child may be entitled. This can be accomplished if the Trustee's power is discretionary and the Trustee can withhold or distribute funds depending on the child's condition and the availability of state or federal funds, within the restrictions imposed by state and federal law.

The Special Needs Trust may contain instructions that surplus income may be accumulated if necessary to avoid disqualification for government benefits. The trust should also contain provisions that prohibit the child from transferring income or principal of the trust to any person.

What about adult family members with special needs?

A Special Needs Trust can also be created to provide for the needs of an adult who is unable to care for himself or herself. All of the previously addressed issues relating to a Special Needs Trust for a child also apply to a Special Needs Trust created for an adult.

CHAPTER FOUR

PROTECTING CHILDREN PHYSICALLY AND FINANCIALLY

THE IMPORTANCE OF
GUARDIANS AND TRUSTEES

Perhaps no other single estate planning issue is more important for parents than making the difficult decision about who will take care of their children if they are unable to care for them themselves. We have learned that for many parents the difficulty of making this decision, due primarily to their inability to select the right person for this critical need, often paralyzes them into not planning at all. We help such parents get over their planning paralysis by pointing out that their failure to plan for their children is itself a choice. By not planning, they are simply abandoning to strangers in a probate court the right to choose who will take care of their children. Loving parents overcome such fears and make these important decisions to protect their children.

How do I choose who will take care of my children if something happens to me?

In planning for children there are two main questions that one must ask. The first question is, "Who will take care of my children's physical needs?" This is the role of a guardian. The second question is, "Who will be responsible for managing the children's inheritance until they are mature enough to manage it themselves?" This is the role of a Trustee. While the roles of a guardian and a Trustee are both important, they require different skills. In order to pick the right person for the right job, it is important to know the duties each performs.

What are the duties of a guardian?

A guardian is responsible for caring for the physical needs of minor children or adults who are disabled. They make decisions involving basic needs such as housing, clothing, medical care, and schooling. For minors, the guardian is the person who will tuck your child in at night. For disabled adults, the guardian is the person who decides if they can be cared for at home or if their condition requires placement in a group home, assisted living facility or nursing home.

How do I choose a guardian?

Choosing a guardian for minors is perhaps the most difficult decision a parent has to make because it is nearly impossible to imagine anyone else doing as good a job as you would do raising your children; however, as pointed out earlier, if you do not choose a guardian for your children, a judge who has no personal knowledge of you or your children will decide who will raise them. Don't allow yourself to become paralyzed trying to find someone who will be as good a parent as you are. That person may not exist. Instead, focus on finding the best person available.

In choosing a guardian for minor children, it is important that you name someone who shares your ideas and values in rearing children. Ask yourself if you and the person you are considering share similar religious beliefs and attitudes toward parental discipline. Ask yourself if they will give your children the same loving care that you give them and will seek to provide them with the same educational opportunities that you would provide.

Another factor that must be considered is the proposed guardian's age. A guardian must not be so young or old that they are unable to care for or cope with very young, adolescent, or teenage children. While age is an important consideration, a number of good candidates are often overlooked merely as a result of their age. Age may be a deciding factor among equally qualified candidates, but it should not automatically disqualify an otherwise appropriate selection.

Many young parents operate under the false assumption that a guardian must be their age or younger. Age has often been cited as a reason *not* to nominate grandparents or others as guardians but a healthy, loving relationship that already exists between children and a potential guardian is the single most important factor to consider when choosing a guardian. If you believe your child would receive love, nurturing, and care from a particular person, that single factor might outweigh any negatives such as age or relocation. In many cultures, the older members of extended families often help raise children. Moreover, grandparents who are overlooked might contest your appointment in court, especially if individuals from outside the family are named.

Also consider the proposed guardian's ability to financially care for your children. If the guardian is not financially equipped to care for your children it may cause an undue burden on the guardian's family and lead to resentment against your children. For this reason, it is wise to consider leaving financial assistance to the guardian to help raise your minor children or help provide for a disabled adult.

You should also consider whether you would want your child raised by a single parent or by a married couple. If you name a couple, you should clearly state what you would want to have happen if there is a death or divorce between the guardians.

Another factor that should be considered in selecting guardians is whether they have children of their own. If they do, ask yourself whether their children will be good playmates for yours. Also ask whether parents who already have children of their own will be able to handle the additional burden, especially since your children may have emotional problems that will require a lot of individual care and attention. Because of these issues, you should not automatically rule out individuals whose children are already grown or who have no children. Sometimes a family with children may better serve as a support network in which all the children can remain friends rather than become sibling rivals.

All of the above issues should be thoroughly discussed with the proposed guardian in order to ensure that the person you select is qualified and to make sure he or she is willing and able to serve. Also, in addition to the primary person you would like to serve as guardian, it is always a good idea to name a backup in case the first person selected is unable to serve. This person is known as a "successor guardian," and can serve if you decide to replace the primary guardian or if the primary guardian is unable or refuses to serve when needed.

How do I nominate and replace a guardian?

You may nominate a guardian for your children in your will. Wills are the legal tool used because the guardian appointment is officially made in probate court. For this reason, individuals with minor children who plan their estates with a living trust should have a will drafted to nominate a guardian.

Since guardians are nominated in a will, the nominated guardian can be replaced simply by signing a new will that nominates a new guardian. Accordingly, a guardian can be changed at any time prior to the disability or death of both parents. After the death of both parents, the guardian can be changed only by court order. Therefore, the appointment of a guardian should be reevaluated on a regular basis as your family needs change and the needs and circumstance of the nominated guardian change.

Once a parent has decided whom to appoint to take care of a child's physical needs, it is next necessary to decide who will be responsible for managing the child's inheritance until he or she is mature enough to manage it. As stated before, this is the responsibility of a Successor Trustee who starts managing the trust if the parent becomes disabled or dies.

Is it important to name a Successor Trustee?

It is important to name a Successor Trustee to prevent the family from having to go through court proceedings to appoint a new Trustee if the Trustmaker is no longer able to serve due to disability or death. The Trustmaker should discuss the appointment with the person to be named so that person will be aware of the duties and responsibilities of a Successor Trustee when the Trustmaker can no longer serve.

What are the duties and responsibilities of a Successor Trustee?

A Successor Trustee's most important duty is to implement the Trust's instructions concerning how the trust property should be used to aid the beneficiaries. Whereas guardians decide how to take care of a beneficiary's physical needs, the Successor Trustee decides how to use trust assets to pay for those needs. Among other responsibilities, a Successor Trustee has the following responsibilities:

- Making an inventory of trust assets;

- Protecting trust assets and making sure they are properly invested;

- Preparing an accounting for beneficiaries;

- Implementing the trustmaker's instructions as to how assets are to be distributed to the beneficiaries or otherwise used for their benefit.

The Successor Trustee need not make these decisions alone. The trust should authorize the Successor Trustee to obtain whatever professional services are necessary to carry out the trust's instructions. Such professionals may include investment advisors, attorneys, insurance agents or certified public accountants.

Each state has statutory guidelines that regulate a trustee's responsibilities. Trustees must use reasonable business judgment in the investment, management, and diversification of the trust assets, taking into account the needs of the beneficiaries. Additionally, trustees must not allow trust assets to be wasted or invest money or other property in speculative or other imprudent investments.

Who can I select to be a Successor Trustee?

A Successor Trustee can be any adult. Possible candidates include family members or friends. Alternately, the services of a professional trustee can be used. These include attorneys, certified public accountants, and trust companies or the trust department of a bank. Selection of a trustee is an important decision and each alternative has advantages and disadvantages.

What are the advantages and disadvantages of selecting a family member or friend as Successor Trustee?

An advantage of selecting family members or friends as Successor Trustees is that they have personal knowledge of the family. Their knowledge of the true needs of the beneficiaries can prove valuable. They can also generally be trusted to act in the beneficiary's best interest and usually will serve for little or no fee. The disadvantages of family members or friends serving as Successor Trustees is that they may make decisions on an emotional, rather than objective basis, and they often lack the financial skills necessary to invest and manage large sums of money.

What are the advantages and disadvantages of selecting an attorney, CPA, or financial advisor as Successor Trustee?

Professional advisors, such as attorneys, CPAs, or financial advisors generally have expertise in finances and knowledge of the legal requirements of trust management. They also usually carry professional liability insurance that financially protects your beneficiaries if mismanagement of trust assets occurs. What professional trustees possess in financial and legal expertise they lack in knowledge of the Trustmaker's family and goals and, with their professional skills come higher fees. Even so, higher fees should not necessarily be a determining factor in choosing a trustee. A professional's fees are often more than compensated for by their ability to obtain for beneficiaries a better return on trust investments.

What are the advantages and disadvantages of selecting a corporate Successor Trustee?

Trust companies or bank trust departments have substantial expertise in serving as trustees, are highly regulated by state and federal agencies, provide professional financial management, and have the financial resources to pay for costly mistakes. The disadvantages of corporate trustees serving as Successor Trustees, as with other professionals, include their higher fees, their lack of knowledge of the Trustmaker's family, and the fact that they are often seen as uncaring and dispassionate. Including instructions in the trust that permit the trustee to be replaced if appropriate can mitigate some of these disadvantages.

How can a trustee be replaced?

The Trustmaker of a revocable trust can change a trustee at any time prior to his or her disability or death by amending the trust to name a new Successor Trustee. The trust can also include instructions that outline the circumstances that allow a Successor

Trustee to be removed. For example, the trust may provide that a majority of the beneficiaries can appoint a new Successor Trustee for specific reasons or for no reason at all. Also, there does not have to be just one Successor Trustee named. Multiple Successor Trustees may be named to serve simultaneously.

Should more than one Successor Trustee be named?

The decision to choose more than one Successor Trustee to serve simultaneously may be based on several factors. Often one person possesses all the necessary skills to serve alone. If this is not the case, co-trustees can be appointed and trust responsibilities divided between them. For example, the Trustee that personally knows the beneficiaries the best can be assigned the responsibility of deciding when to distribute trust assets for their benefit. The Trustee that is most adept at financial matters can be assigned the responsibility for deciding how to invest trust assets. If co-trustees are appointed, the trust agreement should state the specific responsibilities of each Trustee and how joint decisions are to be made.

Another benefit of naming multiple co-trustees is that if one of them resigns, becomes disabled, or dies, the other co-trustee is already in place to continue the trust administration without any interruption. Without this protection, the beneficiaries must deal with the burden of deciding whom to appoint as a Successor Trustee.

A final benefit of naming co-trustees is that they can monitor each other so that trust assets are managed and distributed as the Trustmaker intended. Many believe that it is simply good policy to make sure that multiple individuals are jointly responsible for the trust's administration as it can help prevent the mismanagement, misuse, or theft of the trust's assets.

CHAPTER FIVE

POWERS OF ATTORNEY FOR FINANCES AND PROPERTY

Although a Revocable Trust empowers the trustee to manage property owned by the trust, this is the start and not the end of a sound estate plan. Remember that Revocable Trusts exercise legal control only over property owned by the trust; therefore, additional legal tools are still needed to grant authority to others to manage property outside of the trust and to make legal decisions that do not involve the trust. Otherwise, even with a Revocable Trust, the family could lose control over some of its legal affairs. A Powers of Attorney for Finances and Property is one such tool that helps keep the family in control.

What is a Power of Attorney?

In a Power of Attorney you ("the principal") name a chosen "agent" to exercise legal authority on your behalf the same as if you were doing it yourself. The authority granted can be whatever rights you desire the agent to exercise over your legal affairs and your property. Such authority can include making deposits and withdrawals from your bank accounts, managing your investments, selling your home, or anything else you could do yourself.

Typically such Powers of Attorney take legal effect immediately. Also, the legal authority granted the agent in all Powers of Attorney terminates at the principal's death and usually also terminates if the principal becomes mentally disabled.

What if I want my agent to act for me even if I become disabled?

As stated above, the legal authority granted your agent to act for you in most Powers of Attorney automatically terminates if you become mentally disabled; thus a Power of Attorney can become useless exactly when it is needed the most. For this reason, many Powers of Attorney contain language that makes them "durable" so that the legal authority granted the agent continues even if the principal becomes disabled.

With a Durable Power of Attorney, your agent will continue to have the legal authority to make decisions for you regardless of any subsequent illness, accident or other disabling condition you suffer.

The granting of such legal authority to others is one way that an individual can avoid otherwise necessary guardianship court proceedings. The ability of the family to prevent court proceedings by having a Powers of Attorney in place, and the relatively low cost in having an attorney draft one, makes Powers of Attorney a popular estate planning tool.

Are there any problems associated with Powers of Attorney?

Although Powers of Attorney may be inexpensive to set up initially, they tend to suffer from a number of shortcomings. First, if you believe that an important element of estate planning is to maintain control of your property while you are alive and well, the traditional Power of Attorney might not be acceptable to you because most Powers of Attorney give the agent immediate legal power to act on your behalf even though you neither presently need nor want any help.

This shortcoming can be avoided by using a "Springing" Power of Attorney. Unlike most Powers of Attorney that give the agent the right to act for you immediately, a Springing Power of Attorney allows the agent to act for you only after you become disabled.

Second, even the best Power of Attorney may not work just when you need it the most – when you become disabled and can no longer legally make your own financial decisions. This shortcoming occurs with great frequency because many banks and other financial institutions are extremely rigid and will accept only their own in-house Power of Attorney form. They simply refuse to accept a Power of Attorney drafted by anyone other than their own attorney.

Moreover, just the mere passage of time from the date you sign your Power of Attorney until the time it is used by your agent, may be enough to cause problems. Financial institutions are often concerned that the passage of time has rendered your

Power of Attorney "stale." An old Power of Attorney runs the risk of becoming stale due to the possibility that many things may have changed in your life since you signed it, and the Power no longer truly reflects your present desires.

Rather than risk a lawsuit by honoring a stale Power of Attorney, the financial institution may require a court to establish the validity of the Power of Attorney. Although in most circumstances your agent will win in court, your family will have lost because the whole point of having a Power of Attorney was to avoid a trip to the courthouse in the first place. This problem with "stale" Powers of Attorney is why it is sound advice to update them every couple years, or even more often.

A third shortcoming of Financial Powers of Attorney often arises when not enough legal authority is granted the agent. For example, the typical Power of Attorney gives your agent control over all your assets, including the right to sell your real estate but the document is entirely silent about the agent's legal ability to use the proceeds of that sale for your benefit.

It is important to leave detailed instructions about how the proceeds from the sale of your property are to be used if you are disabled. Are such proceeds to be used only for your own benefit?

Alternately, is your agent authorized to also use your property to take care of others that you are currently helping, such as aging parents or your minor or adult children who may find themselves in financial or medical difficulties? While such instructions in a Power of Attorney give needed authority to your agent, they simultaneously contribute to the difficulty of getting a financial institution or other third party to honor it.

Conversely, a fourth shortcoming of Financial Powers of Attorney is the danger of giving the agent too much legal authority. Unfortunately, the legal treatises are full of instances where agents used their power to wrongfully abscond with all of the principal's property.

For all of the above reasons, although Powers of Attorney offer valuable estate-planning opportunities, they also embody several significant shortcomings. Foremost among these is that they dangerously grant the agent broad legal authority over the principal's property with little in the way of detailed instructions or restrictions to prevent the abuse of that power. The reality is that many times Powers of Attorney are used in an attempt to accomplish more than is wise or prudent.

Fortunately, there is a ready solution to this dilemma. Instead of using Powers of Attorney to grant an agent legal authority to do everything imaginable, a much better approach is to use a Power of Attorney that grants only limited authority in conjunction with a comprehensive estate plan that has at its center a Revocable Living Trust.

Powers of Attorney created for limited and specific purposes can be of great value in estate planning when used with a Revocable Living Trust. For example, as the estate planning centerpiece, the Revocable Living Trust will accomplish what it is expressly designed to do – help the estate escape guardianship proceedings while also providing the Trustee with detailed instructions that authorize only appropriate use of trust funds to help you and your loved ones and no one else.

The Power of Attorney then supplements this authority by authorizing the agent to handle any property or legal issue not controlled by the trust. Such legal issues could include representing you if you become injured in an automobile accident, advocating for you before government agencies, and dealing with insurance or retirement account issues. Other limited powers could include the authority to transfer assets to your trust but not give them away. Using a Revocable Living Trust with a Power of Attorney, you will be more secure in the knowledge that the instructions you leave will actually work as you intend without court intervention or the risk of being victimized by an unscrupulous agent.

CHAPTER SIX

HEALTHCARE POWERS OF ATTORNEY AND "LIVING WILLS"

While a Revocable Living Trust and Power of Attorney are valuable tools for handling property and financial issues, they do nothing to answer another very important planning question— who will make healthcare decisions for you if you are mentally disabled and unable to make those decisions for yourself? The legal tools used to answer that question are known as "health care directives," of which there are two types: Healthcare Powers of Attorney and "Living Wills."

What is a Healthcare Power of Attorney?

All states have laws that authorize you to create a special Power of Attorney in which you designate an agent to make health care decisions for you if you are unable to do so yourself. These Healthcare Powers of Attorney can also be used to provide instructions to your agent concerning the type of care you do or do not want to receive if disabled, seriously ill, or injured.

It is important to get professional advice when preparing a Healthcare Power of Attorney because each state has its own requirements for how the document is to be signed, how many agents may be used at any given time, and restrictions on the types of medical decisions that may or may not be made by an agent. Also, because the person you appoint as your healthcare agent could literally have life and death decision-making authority over you, selection of an agent should be done with the utmost care.

The person you select for your healthcare agent should be someone who not only knows you well, but also understands your views about continuing health care in circumstances where you are terminally ill or suffering from a permanent loss of consciousness. Remember, these are decisions of the heart and don't necessarily require the same financial skills you might want to see in a trustee. In fact, the person who is the best with a dollar may be the very last person you would want making these life and death decisions for you.

Your spouse, other family members, or close friends are usually good candidates to be the healthcare agent. But whomever you chose, it is important that you thoroughly discuss with your agent your desires concerning whether you should receive or refuse healthcare services under various situations.

Your estate planning attorney should be able to provide you with a list of questions that will address these issues which you can then review with your intended healthcare agent.

What is a Living Will?

In addition to statutes authorizing you to appoint a healthcare agent, most states have statutes that authorize you to leave instructions concerning the specific types of treatments you do or do not want to receive. These instructions are generically known as "Living Wills," and in some states known by their more technical legal definition, "Declarations To Physicians."

Living Wills, in essence, are intended to provide you with a way to express in advance your desires concerning your health care treatment. They are mainly used by those who desire to authorize the withdrawal of life sustaining care if their treating physician's medical diagnosis is that continuing healthcare is simply prolonging their life without hope of meaningful recovery. Living Wills can also be used to provide instructions about the types of medical treatment the patient does not want withheld or withdrawn.

Ordinarily, Living Wills require the agreement of two physicians that the conditions you have identified to withdraw care have, in fact, occurred. For example, before the healthcare provider can "pull the plug", two physicians must agree that you are suffering from a terminal condition or that you are in a "persistent vegetative state."

Which Healthcare Directive should I have?

Recently, there has been a good deal of concern that health professionals frequently do not follow the directives contained in

Living Wills because either the healthcare professionals did not know the patient had a Living Will or because the patient's instructions were ignored under a "doctor knows best" philosophy. Also, in most states the care instructions provided in a Healthcare Power of Attorney override the instructions left in a Living Will if the two conflict with each other.

For these reasons, many estate planners recommend that the primary healthcare directive be the appointment of a specific healthcare agent in a Healthcare Power of Attorney. A handpicked agent serving as your healthcare advocate could make the difference between whether your healthcare instructions will be followed or not.

On the other hand, some estate planners argue that also having a Living Will in place can provide needed instructions if your healthcare agent, for any reason, is unable to serve. This is usually not a problem because of your ability to appoint successor healthcare agents if the first one named does not serve. Ultimately, the decision whether to have one or both documents is an important issue to discuss with your estate planning attorney.

Are there any other healthcare issues to consider?

Many of our clients spend portions of the year in different states. If you live part-time in another state you may wish to have your healthcare directives prepared in each of your states of residence. Healthcare directives are mostly state specific. If you desire to have your wishes carried out no matter where you are if you become ill or injured, it is advisable to have a healthcare directive that complies with the law of all states where you reside a significant portion of the year.

Also, it is important to let others know that you have healthcare directives. Once prepared and signed, you should give copies of your healthcare directives to your chosen agents as well as your family physician.

There are also professional services, such as Docubank or U.S. Living Will Registry, that offer twenty-four hour worldwide availability of your healthcare directives with only a phone call. Your estate planning attorney can help arrange for these services if desired.

You should also ask your estate planning attorney if there are any other unusual provisions in your state's laws of which you should be made aware. For example, in some states you may be able to obtain a "do not resuscitate" bracelet that instructs paramedics and other healthcare professionals that you do not want to receive resuscitation services if you cannot communicate that desire yourself.

What is HIPAA and how does it affect me?

Congress enacted the Health Insurance Portability and Accountability Act of 1996 (HIPAA) to protect your healthcare information. The primary objective is to ensure the electronic transmission of health care information between insurance companies remains private. A consequence of these strict privacy rules is that your healthcare provider may be prevented from sharing healthcare information with your loved ones.

HIPAA imposes significant penalties on health care providers who release your information without proper authorization. To avoid a situation where your family is unable to obtain necessary healthcare information when an emergency arises, it is imperative that you have either a Healthcare Power of Attorney or specific HIPAA compliant authorizations permitting the release of your healthcare information to the people you have specified.

CHAPTER SEVEN

ESTATE PLANNING FOR MARRIED COUPLES – SEPARATE PROPERTY VERSUS COMMUNITY PROPERTY

There are two systems of property ownership in the United States that affect the property owned by married couples: separate property and community property. The state in which the property is located determines which of these two systems legally govern a married couple's property. Separate property law governs any property owned by married couples residing in separate property states. Community property law governs property owned by married couples residing in community property states. The community property states are Alaska, Arizona, California, Idaho, Louisiana, Nevada, New Mexico, Texas, Washington and Wisconsin.

In states that use the separate property system, the name on the title determines which spouse owns that property. For example, in most separate property states, a paycheck issued in the name of the wife is the wife's individual property. If she uses her paycheck to purchase real estate that is titled just in her name, legally that real estate is hers alone and she can do with it as she pleases without her spouse's permission.

Conversely, in community property states, the name on the title does not necessarily determine the ownership of a married couple's property. For example, a wife who receives a paycheck in a community property state does not own all of it as her own separate property. Instead, half of the paycheck is owned by her husband. If she uses her paycheck to buy some real estate, that real estate will be the community property of both spouses, even though only the wife's name is on the title. When property is owned as community property, each spouse has a half interest in the property. There can be important legal consequences depending on which system of property ownership controls your property.

What are some of the legal consequences of owning property separately rather than as community property?

The way your property is classified is important because there are several estate planning advantages for married couples that own property in a community property state that do not exist for couples living in separate property states. The first involves a capital gains tax benefit.

Couples that own community property that has appreciated in value, and for which a capital gains tax would ordinarily be due when it is sold, receive what is known as a double step-up in its tax basis at the death of the first spouse. The benefit of this double step-up in basis becomes apparent when one calculates the capital gains taxes otherwise due as a result of the property's appreciation. The double step-up in tax basis will quite often enable the surviving spouse to escape capital gains taxes entirely because the starting point in calculating the property's appreciation is the date of the first spouse's death—not the date the couple originally purchased the property. Assets sold immediately after the death of the first spouse will show no taxable appreciation.

A brief example shows how this works. Suppose a married couple in a separate property state jointly owned some stock they had purchased ten years ago for two dollars. The two dollars becomes the starting point, or tax "basis," for calculating any taxable appreciation in the stock's value. Let's say that during those ten years the stock appreciated in value to twenty dollars. If the stock were sold while both spouses were living, a capital gains tax would be imposed on the eighteen dollars profit.

Now assume the husband of that couple died before the sale. If the jointly owned stock was sold after his death, the tax laws give a step-up in basis for the decedent husband's half of the property, but no step-up for the surviving wife's share. This means that if the stock were sold for twenty dollars the day after the husband died, there would be a step-up in basis from one dollar (the husband's one-half of the original two-dollar basis) to ten dollars (his one-half of the twenty dollar sale price). But no step-up occurs on his surviving wife's half interest. Accordingly, upon the sale she will be required to pay a capital gains tax on the nine dollars profit attributable to her half of the stock.

Compare this to the result that would occur if the couple lived in a community property state where they would own the stock together as community property. When the husband died, not only would his half of the property receive a step-up in basis but hers would be stepped up as well, even though she is still living. This is the meaning of the term *double step-up in basis*. Due to this double step-up in basis, the property's tax basis becomes its fair market value on the date of the husband's death. If the property's basis is twenty dollars when the husband dies, and the wife thereafter sells it for twenty dollars, there is technically no profit on the twenty-dollar sale and thus no capital gains tax is owed. This can be a huge tax benefit for couples that own significant amounts of appreciated assets.

Are there any other differences between separate and community property?

Another distinct advantage of community property ownership is that it works well for couples that wish to reduce or eliminate estate taxes. To avoid such taxation, property is transferred at the death of the first spouse to a tax sheltered Family Trust (also referred to as a Credit Shelter Trust or Bypass Trust), rather than directly to the surviving spouse where it would be taxable in that spouse's estate.

Community property works well for this type of estate tax planning because it tends to equalize the value of the estate owned by each spouse. In community property states like Wisconsin, even if only the husband's name appears on the title, one half of it (with some exceptions) is still considered legally owned by the wife; therefore, regardless of which spouse dies first, there are assets to transfer to the tax-sheltered family trust.

A different situation occurs in a separate property state when couples have all of the property titled only in the name of the husband. The husband is viewed as the owner of that property not only for purposes of passing on the property at death, but also for the imposition of estate taxes. This situation can cause a major tax problem if the wife dies first. Since everything is legally titled in her husband's name, there will be no property from the wife's estate to transfer to the tax-sheltered Family Trust. The opportunity this couple had to reduce estate taxes is lost forever.

In separate property states, the problem of one spouse individually owing the bulk of their combined assets can be solved by gifting selected assets from the spouse with the larger estate to the spouse with the smaller estate. This swap of assets continues until both spouses own assets in the amount needed to fund the Family Trust regardless of who dies first. A downside to this strategy is that if appreciated assets are gifted to the spouse who ends up the survivor, there is no step-up in basis at the death of the first spouse and thus no capital gains tax savings.

Are there other differences?

Community property ownership also provides another estate tax planning advantage over separate property. Unless specifically provided for, a community property spouse has no survivorship rights, other than a homestead. The deceased spouse's half of the property may be transferred to a tax-sheltered Family Trust without the risk that the transfer will be defeated by an automatic transfer to the surviving spouse. This is contrary to a separate property system where if a couple owns property in both names, the surviving spouse automatically owns all such property. The unfortunate result is that no property remains to be transferred to a tax-sheltered Family Trust. Couples intending to reduce estate taxes in separate property states must carefully weigh the estate tax consequences of joint tenancy ownership of property.

A final benefit of owning property in a community property state is that individuals living there can choose for themselves which property system they desire for part or all of their property. They can classify their property as community, separate, or a mix of the two depending on their individual circumstances and desires. These options may best be handled by creating a Community Property Agreement when permitted under state law.

What is a Community Property Agreement?

A Community Property Agreement is a contract that a married couple in a community property state sign as a couple that specifies how they want their property to be classified. Classification may be as community property or separate property, or a mix of the two. It is very important that couples in community property states take advantage of the opportunity to prepare a Community Property Agreement. Otherwise due to the complexity of the law, it can be very difficult to know exactly how your property is classified, and unless you know how it is classified you cannot know with certainty how it will pass at your death.

As stated in Chapter One, the fundamental principal in estate planning is that a person may only transfer what he or she owns. In a community property state, a married person owns only one-half of the community property and all of his or her individual property. Distinguishing community property from individual property can be a rather complex exercise.

Community property states use a complicated formula used to determine how much of a mixed property account balance is community and how much is individual. This formula is applied at the first spouse's death to determine how much of the mixed property account belongs to the surviving spouse as community property. This calculation is critical for estate planning purposes because the deceased spouse is legally entitled to pass on only his or her own property to beneficiaries other than the surviving spouse.

The complexity of these issues frequently cause Community Property Agreements to be used to classify in advance all of the couple's property as individual or community in order to simplify the process at the first spouse's death and save costs. There are pros and cons to classifying property as individual or community and deciding which classification is best often entails an asset-by-asset inquiry by an experienced estate planning attorney.

One advantage of classifying your property as community is that it will receive the beneficial double step-up in its tax basis at the first spouse's death, but there are other factors to consider. In some cases, a couple may want to forgo the capital gains tax benefits of community property and instead classify property as individual to accomplish other estate planning goals. Such possible goals could include the following:

- They wish to provide for children of a prior marriage;

- One spouse has a large family inheritance; or

- One spouse has exposure to creditor claims and wishes to protect the other spouse from such claims.

In summary, a sound estate plan for married couples must always take into account the specific laws of the state they live in. There are important estate planning decisions that must be made whether one lives in a separate property state, or in a community property state. Your estate planning attorney can assist you in explaining these complicated matters to help you maximize your estate planning opportunities and give you confidence that you know exactly how your estate will pass at your death.

CHAPTER EIGHT

SUCCESSION PLANNING FOR THE FAMILY-OWNED BUSINESS OR FARM

In addition to the estate planning challenges facing us all, those who have family-owned businesses or farms have additional succession and planning challenges to confront. The farm or business is often a valuable family asset that must be factored into the family's overall estate plan. Planning for a smooth and successful transition of the business to the next generation is critical if a lifetime of effort is to be preserved.

Why is planning for the family owned business important?

Family owned businesses form the backbone of American enterprise, but surveys of small business owners reveal that little or no planning for survival of the business to the next generation has been accomplished. The importance of family owned business is evident from statistics which reveal that over the past decade, all net job growth in the United States has occurred in businesses with 20 or fewer employees. Estimates from the Internal Revenue Service suggest that 95% of U.S. corporations are closely-held and that they account for over one-half of the gross national product along with 50% of the total wages paid.

While nearly 70% of the family owned or closely-held business owners express the desire to have the business remain under family ownership, less than 1/3 of business owners have established formal business succession plans. Children frequently come into the business with inadequate skills or training, as nearly 85% of the children of family business owners become involved in the family business directly from school without obtaining other work experience. With these statistics, it is understandable that only 35% of family businesses pass successfully to the next generation and less than 13% of these businesses stay in the family for a period in excess of 60 years. For family owned businesses to accomplish successful transfer to the next generation, appropriate planning is essential.

What causes business succession planning to fail?

Depending upon the desires of the family, succession planning may involve the sale of the business to outsiders or passing the business on to the next generation. Given the impact of estate taxes, a business owner must either create equity to pay the estate taxes at the time of death or wealth transfer planning must be undertaken during life.

Succession planning with a closely held business creates its challenges because of the inherent nature of such businesses.

Typically, a family owned business centers its goodwill around the efforts of a key individual, who is typically the founder. Upon the death or retirement of this individual, the business may lack successor management or the charismatic flavor that has made the business successful.

Other reasons why the business succession fails in the majority of instances usually center around the failure to plan and include procrastination in planning by the business owners, failure to plan for the payment of estate and/or income taxes, failure to arrange for funds to provide for the retirement of the founding member while continuing to support the business in the manner in which it can be successful, reluctance of other family members to come into the business, leaving the business without a successor, and family disputes concerning control or ownership.

When lifetime planning is not done, negotiations may have to be accomplished upon the death or withdrawal of an owner, which may lead to family acrimony. Uncertainty as to the parents' desires and plans concerning decision-making authority and division of profits may cause emotional issues that cannot be overcome. Death taxes may be incurred which would otherwise be unnecessary, and ownership may have to be transferred to an unsuitable outsider.

How should you establish your succession plan?

A proper business succession plan will provide for the survival and continuity of the business. It should minimize income and estate taxes, and it should also promote family relations through the fair treatment of all the children and identification of the expected decision-making process.

The first step in formulating a successful family business succession plan is to assemble the succession planning team. In addition to the appropriate family members, professional services of your attorney, accountant, financial planner, and insurance professional are required. Each team member brings different knowledge and expertise to the table. Participation by the family is of utmost importance to identify the planning goals of the family. These goals form the crux of the planning, and may include such issues as the maintenance of jobs for children, holding on to managerial control, or the transfer of control to specific family members. The establishment of the goals provides the highway upon which the planning team will travel.

A thorough analysis of the status of the business needs to be undertaken, including historic financial documentation. Legal documents must also be reviewed, including Shareholder and/ or Partnership Agreements, Employment Contracts, Articles of Incorporation, IRS elections, Marital Property Agreements, Wills, Trust Agreements, and Deferred Compensation Agreements. Estate and wealth transfer taxes need to be projected and planned for. Once the succession team has identified the plan, it needs to be shared with the family and then implemented.

CHAPTER NINE

THE IRREVOCABLE LIFE INSURANCE TRUST

A common misconception is that life insurance proceeds are entirely tax-free. While it is true that life insurance proceeds are generally free from income taxes, many people are both surprised and dismayed when they learn that their life insurance proceeds are subject to estate taxation.

To understand why life insurance proceeds are subject to an estate tax, we must first understand that the estate tax is a transfer tax. The Internal Revenue Service (IRS) taxes the transfer of wealth from one person to another—transfers during life are subject to a gift tax and transfers at death are subject to an estate tax. When you die all of your property (including life insurance proceeds) will be taxed when it is transferred to your beneficiaries. In addition, the IRS will tax the death benefits of any life insurance policy in which you have an "incident of ownership." An incident of ownership includes any right to change the beneficiary of the policy or the right to borrow against its cash value.

Nonetheless, life insurance is an extraordinaryly helpful estate planning tool. It can provide critically needed funds to replace the income lost if the family's breadwinner dies. It can also preserve an estate by providing the liquidity needed to pay estate taxes. Without it, the family home, farm, or business might have to be sold to pay those taxes.

Despite these benefits, owning a life insurance policy poses one major estate planning challenge: although it will offer your family needed financial security, it will also simultaneously increase the size of your taxable estate. In other words, the death benefit of your life insurance policy might itself result in additional estate taxes that must be paid.

Can you explain more about taxes on life insurance?

As stated above, the IRS taxes all of the property that we transfer to others whether while we are still alive or at the time of our deaths; however, there are a few exceptions to this transfer tax. One such exemption is that under current tax laws every American citizen can transfer to others a certain amount of their property tax-free. The amount of property that you can transfer tax-free is known as the "exclusion" amount and is determined year to year by Congress. These taxes have been higher than fifty percent of the taxable estate value. The addition of life insurance proceeds can, and often do, push estates over the exclusion amount. When this happens, otherwise tax free estates become subject to estate taxation simply because of the existence of the life insurance. The result is that a large portion of the life insurance goes to pay estate taxes instead of to the beneficiaries. Since the exclusion amount is frequently changed by Congress, you should see a qualified estate planning attorney to learn the current amounts and to determine if your life insurance is rendering your estate taxable.

Is there a way for me to protect my life insurance from estate taxes?

Although owning life insurance can add to the tax burden on your estate, there is a solution to this problem. The solution is to place your life insurance into a special trust known as an Irrevocable Life Insurance Trust (ILIT).

What is an ILIT?

An ILIT is similar to all trusts in that assets transferred to it are administered by a trustee who is required to follow the trust instructions. However, unlike *revocable* trusts that are usually established for the Trustmaker's benefit and which can be amended by the Trustmaker at any time and for any reason, an ILIT is established for the benefit of someone *other than the Trustmaker*, usually the Trustmaker's spouse or children. Furthermore, once created ILITs usually cannot be amended, at least not without the permission of a court of law. Neither of these limitations, though, is usually significant in light of the great planning opportunities available with an ILIT.

What planning opportunities do ILITs provide?

An ILIT accomplishes two objectives. First, it removes life insurance death proceeds from your estate and thereby reduces the value of your estate for estate tax purposes. Second, it allows you to direct how the proceeds of your life insurance will pass to your beneficiaries.

A brief example shows how an ILIT can prevent your life insurance from triggering unnecessary estate taxes. As stated earlier, if at the time of your death your property (including life insurance) exceeds the exclusion amount, your estate will have to pay estate taxes; however, if the life insurance is removed from your taxable estate by transferring it to an ILIT, the taxable value of your estate will decrease by the amount of the life insurance removed from it. The smaller your taxable estate the smaller your estate tax burden.

The best thing about ILITs is that they are specially designed to hold life insurance tax-free. The life insurance death proceeds will pass to your chosen beneficiaries estate tax-free because it was owned by the trust – not by you. It is that simple.

Does this sound too good to be true? It is not if the ILIT is properly drafted and implemented! In order to achieve this re-markable result, the ILIT must be drafted very carefully, the life insurance policies must be transferred to the ILIT in a specific manner, and the life insurance premiums must be paid in the cor-rect fashion. Good advice from an experienced estate planning attorney is essential to making sure each of these detailed steps, and others, are done correctly.

What other details are involved with creating an ILIT?

One important detail in creating an ILIT is the selection of the trustee. Unlike revocable trusts where you can be your own trustee, you cannot be the trustee of your own ILIT. The IRS will treat the life insurance as if it is still in your own taxable estate because you will have too much personal control over it. Your spouse or adult child may be the trustee, but because of the technical requirements of ILITs, a better choice might be your accountant, another professional advisor, or a bank or trust company. The choice of your trustee should be given careful consideration.

Another important detail involving ILITs concerns the transfer of the life insurance policy to the trust. You can transfer either existing policies into your ILIT or you can have your trustee purchase a new life insurance policy that insures your life but is owned by the trust.

If you transfer an existing policy into an ILIT, there are two cautions. The transfer of an existing policy to an ILIT is treated under the tax code as a taxable gift, with the potential to trigger gift taxes. Whether or not the gift of an existing policy is taxable depends on the value of the policy and the amount of the current gift tax exemption. The other drawback of transferring an existing policy to an ILIT is that if you die within three years of the transfer, the IRS will consider the transfer invalid and the policy will be still included in your taxable estate.

These limitations make it preferable to purchase a new policy if you are still insurable. If a new policy is purchased, you will not have to be concerned with either determining an existing policy's value for gift tax purposes or with the three-year transfer rule. Many clients are not concerned about the small statistical chance of dying within three years of the transfer. They consider the opportunity to save sometimes hundreds of thousands of dollars of their life insurance well worth the risk and the cost of establishing the ILIT.

When a new life insurance policy is transferred to an ILIT, the ILIT becomes responsible for paying the premiums necessary to keep it in force. The ILIT receives the funds needed to pay such premiums by accepting cash gifts from you or others. When these gifts are made, special care must be taken to ensure that no adverse federal gift taxes are incurred. It would be pointless to avoid estate taxes only to incur gift taxes. Careful planning is needed to simultaneously avoid both gift and estate taxes.

Can't I just give my life insurance policy to someone instead of creating an ILIT?

Questions frequently asked are, "Is it really necessary to go through all of the steps needed to create and transfer life insurance to an ILIT? Wouldn't it simply be easier to remove the insurance from my taxable estate by gifting the policy to my spouse or another family member?" Although gifting a life insurance policy to someone else to remove it from your taxable estate is possible, there are a myriad of problems with someone else owning your policy.

First, when the policy is transferred to an individual, the same gift tax consequences must be considered that exist when transferring it to an ILIT. The steps taken in creating an ILIT make sure these gift tax issues are not overlooked.

Second, if a spouse or adult child owns a policy on your life, and he or she dies first, the policy's value may cause an estate tax problem in his or her estate. Using an ILIT can significantly reduce or even eliminate the estate tax specter—not merely shift the tax burden from one person to another.

Third, when you transfer a life insurance policy to another person you lose all legal control over it. The new owner can change the beneficiary, take the cash value, or even cancel the insurance. Creating an ILIT where your chosen trustee is required to follow your instructions concerning use of trust assets can prevent this. A trustee will be responsible for paying premiums and is more likely to keep the policy in force than would a child or children when called upon to write a check for the premium.

Fourth, when insurance is transferred to individuals, the beneficiaries usually receive the proceeds as an outright distribution at your death. Your family would lose all of the distribution protections that exist when life insurance is transferred to an ILIT. These protections include the following:

- If your children are underage they cannot accept ownership of any death benefits. If a minor child is named as a beneficiary of a life insurance policy, the insurance company will not pay the proceeds to the child. It will instead force the matter into probate court where the court will probaby order the proceeds held in trust until the child's eighteenth birthday. The child will then receive a cashier's check for the remaining balance. This would not happen with an ILIT, which would allow you to maintain control over when and how children receive the proceeds;

- The death of a trust beneficiary will not result in the premature transfer of the policy to his or her spouse or minor child;

- Children may have asset protection from creditors, lawsuits, and divorcing spouses when life insurance is placed in an ILIT;

- An ILIT guarantees that the administrator of your estate will have liquidity needed to pay expenses and coordinate the administration of your estate;

- ILITs permit the use of generation-skipping transfers, a method used to pass unspent proceeds of the insurance from generation to generation without incurring taxes, that are not available with an outright distribution.

Creating an ILIT that meets your objectives and fits into your overall estate plan requires careful planning and the assistance of an insurance professional and estate planning attorney. If properly established and implemented, it is an excellent way to help create an estate, protect an estate from unnecessary taxation, and most importantly, provide a lasting legacy for your loved ones.

CHAPTER TEN

ADVANCED ESTATE PLANNING WITH IRREVOCABLE TRUSTS

The previous chapter reviewed the many advantages of using an Irrevocable Life Insurance Trust (ILIT) to plan for and protect your family. ILITs are just one of several types of irrevocable trusts that are available to meet your estate planning needs. Other types of irrevocable trusts also exist that in the right circumstances could provide great benefits to you and your family. Like ILITs, these irrevocable trusts are designed to save either all or a part of the estate taxes otherwise due on the assets conveyed into them.

Unlike ILITs which are designed to benefit your family but not you, these special irrevocable trusts allow you, under certain IRS restrictions, to gift an asset out of your taxable estate but still personally benefit from it during your life.

How can I remove property from my taxable estate and still personally benefit from it?

Individuals with large taxable estates often own assets that rapidly appreciate in value. To save estate taxes, these appreciating assets must be eliminated from the gross taxable estate. Often these assets offer benefits like the ability to live in your home or generate considerable income that the owner cannot or does not want to relinquish. Also, the gift tax consequences of simply giving these assets away may be prohibitive.

The solution to this problem is to convey such appreciating assets to an irrevocable trust that contains special instructions. Those instructions state that at your death the trust's assets will belong to your designated beneficiaries; therefore the assets will not be a part of your taxable estate when you die. Just as important, the instructions also state that you reserve the right for a specified number of years to still use and benefit from the property transferred to the trust. An advanced estate plan that includes an irrevocable trust can empower you to personally benefit from your property while still removing it from your taxable estate. Additionally, the asset transferred to the trust might be entitled to a valuation discount.

What kind of valuation discounts do irrevocable trusts offer?

One benefit of advanced planning with irrevocable trusts is that the property transferred to the trust is often entitled to a valuation discount for gift tax purposes. This valuation discount is given because the beneficiaries of the trust will not receive its benefits for many years; thus the assets transferred to the trust are significantly less valuable to the beneficiaries than if the beneficiaries received them immediately.

The value of the assets transferred to the trust (for gift tax purposes) is therefore something less than their present fair market value. The end result of such valuation discounts is that more property can be transferred to the irrevocable trust without exceeding the amount you can transfer free of gift taxes each year.

The calculated value of the discount when assets are transferred to an irrevocable trust is based on several factors. These include how much income or other benefit the Trustmaker will personally receive from the trust, how long the Trustmaker will benefit from the trust's property, and the current interest rates. The more the Trustmaker personally benefits from the trust, the less value it has to the ultimate beneficiaries and therefore the less its value for gift tax purposes.

There are many creative ways for you to benefit from the assets transferred to an irrevocable trust. One such way to benefit is to reserve for yourself the right to continue living in your home even after it is transferred to the trust. These types of irrevocable trusts are known as Qualified Personal Residence Trusts (QPRTs).

Can you describe how a Qualified Personal Residence Trust works?

Suppose you have a taxable estate and a significant part of it consists of your personal residence or a vacation home. One way to reduce your taxable estate would be to immediately gift one of these to your children; however doing so might be undesirable because you would then lose control over it (and you still want to live there), and because you would also incur significant gift taxes.

The solution is to transfer your home or cottage to a QPRT. The QPRT's instructions state that you will be entitled to use it for a predetermined amount of time after which ownership of it will transfer to your children. This will insure your continued right to live there, remove it from your taxable estate, and also entitle the asset to a valuation discount, which will lighten the gift tax burden. A similar strategy with similar results is available for those with income producing assets.

Can you describe how an irrevocable tust can benefit those with income producing assets?

If instead of an expensive home, assume that you have an asset that is producing considerable annual income. If you die owning the asset, it will cause an estate tax problem. If you simply transfer it to the children immediately you would lose the annual income (which you still need), and also cause a gift tax problem. One solution is to transfer the asset to an irrevocable trust containing instructions that you will continue receiving income for a specified number of years after which time it will be given to your named beneficiaries. You will continue receiving income even though the asset will be out of your taxable estate.

You might again be entitled to a valuation discount for gift tax purposes, depending on your specific situation. For this reason, advanced planning with irrevocable trusts can be a powerful estate planning tool.

What else should I know about advanced planning with irrevocable trusts?

It is important to understand that in order to work properly, the advanced estate planning strategies discussed in this chapter must comply fully with very technical provisions of the tax code. Accordingly, this type of planning should only be entrusted to an attorney that concentrates his practice in this area of the law. Advanced estate planning involving irrevocable trusts is definitely not the type of legal work to entrust to someone who does not specialize in this area of the law.

CHAPTER ELEVEN

DYNASTY TRUSTS

It was once possible for wealthy individuals to entirely avoid federal estate taxation by placing assets in trusts that established life estates for children and each succeeding generation. This strategy completely circumvented federal estate taxes because the tax code then taxed only property that an individual had a right to give away at death. Since these trusts gave the children and later generations only the right to use the inheritance during their own lives (a life estate), but not the right to name who received any part of the untouched trust assets still remaining at their deaths, no estate tax was ever paid.

Congress ultimately closed this incredible loophole by enacting a law that taxed these "generation skipping" transfers. This tax, known as the Generation Skipping Transfer Tax (GST), is designed to ensure that transfers of assets from one generation to the next cannot escape estate taxation. This tax is especially onerous as it is set at the highest current tax rate.

By assessing a GST tax, the government is attempting to carry out a policy of imposing an estate tax every time wealth passes from one generation to the next; otherwise, an opportunity for taxation is lost. For example, the kind of generation skip which the GST tax is designed to prevent would occur when wealth passes directly from grandparent to grandchild and thereby "skips" an estate tax that would otherwise have occurred if a transfer had been made to the grandparent's own child.

Is there a way to avoid the generation skipping tax?

With good planning, assets may be partially transferred to succeeding generations without triggering the GST. Although it sought to prevent most generation skipping transfers from occurring, Congress decided to give individuals the right to transfer to future generations a limited amount of property free of the GST. In addition to the estate tax exclusion amount, every individual has an equal generation skipping tax exemption.

It is important to realize that the generation skipping tax is imposed *in addition* to the estate tax. If a grandparent attempts to transfer more than the GST exempt amount collectively to the grandchildren, first estate taxes and then GST taxes will be imposed on the transfer. When the two taxes are combined, most of the estate can be consumed by taxes.

The GST exemption available to you provides a wonderful planning opportunity when used in combination with other estate tax planning techniques. That opportunity is called a Dynasty Trust.

What is a Dynasty Trust?

A Dynasty Trust is a special trust established for those who desire to make full use of an individual's right to pass assets to grandchildren or other descendants and thereby skip a generation without the GST being imposed. Since the GST exemption applies to all individuals, married couples can shelter two times the GST exempt amount from GST taxes. This means that if you are married, you and your spouse can leave twice the GST exempt amount in trust for the benefit of succeeding generations in such a way that those assets will never again be subject to estate taxation. The wealth in your Dynasty Trust would then pass from generation to generation estate tax free and provide funds to your descendants for their health, support, and education. The limitation that distributions can only be made for health, support, and education is enough to keep the trust assets out of the beneficiary's estate while providing maintenance of the beneficiary's lifestyle.

Can I create a Dynasty Trust in addition to a Revocable Living Trust?

There is no reason why a Dynasty Trust cannot be incorporated into your individually designed Revocable Living Trust. As is the case with all revocable trusts, the planning opportunities are endless. For example, the Dynasty Trust can provide first for the care of your children and thereafter for your grandchildren and succeeding generations. If you want to prevent the possibility of having the trust assets entirely consumed by your children, you could restrict the use of trust assets by your children to only specific purposes. After the last of your children dies, the remaining trust assets could pass to individual trusts established for each of your grandchildren. This funding pattern could repeat through generations, subject only to the limits of state law on the existence of the trust. Several states have no artificial end to the length of time trusts can exist, and creation of a trust in one of these states can allow a multigenerational trust to last forever.

Apart from providing for your children and grandchildren, Dynasty Trusts can also provide them with asset protection from abusive creditors, lawsuits, and even from failed marriages. The assets generally cannot be taken by outsiders or in divorce proceedings because they are owned by the trust, not by your child or grandchild.

Additionally, as long as the Dynasty Trust does not allow the beneficiary too much access (distributions for a beneficiary's health, education, maintenance and support are acceptable), the assets are never regarded by the IRS as being "owned" by your beneficiaries and are not taxed in their estates. This allows a terrific opportunity for the estate tax-free growth of the assets not used to take care of the beneficiaries.

To see just how powerful estate tax-free compounding of interest can be over an extended period of time, consider the following example: If trust assets grow annually at only six percent, one million dollars grows to over eighty million dollars in the seventy five years it would take for it to pass through three generations. During all of that time your descendants would have comfortable access to interest earnings and could even spend it all if needed (i.e., for a health crisis). Further, if they bought and retained assets in the name of the trust, they would always have the dual benefits of asset protection and estate tax-free growth.

Conversely, assume that your family does not create a Dynasty Trust and the one million dollars similarly grows at six percent over seventy-five years. If each generation is taxed at fifty-five percent, after seventy-five years the money will have grown to be only slightly more than seven million dollars. Using conservative numbers, over a seventy-five year period the difference between using a Dynasty Trust and not using a Dynasty Trust is about seventy-three million dollars!

Are there any other uses of Dynasty Trusts?

A revocable trust is just one of the estate planning tools available to take advantage of Dynasty Trust planning. Irrevocable Life Insurance Trusts provide another vehicle by which parents can use Dynasty Trust planning to benefit their children, grandchildren, or both. If done correctly, the generation skipping tax exemption can be applied to the money gifted to the ILIT and used to pay the insurance premiums. In this scenario, the amount of the GST exemption used up is the amount of the gifts used to pay the life insurance premium and not the insurances death benefit. For example, if a grandparent gifted one hundred thousand dollars to an Irrevocable Life Insurance Trust established to benefit the grandchildren, the ILIT Trustee could use it to purchase a life insurance policy worth several times the gift. The GST exemption would then be used to offset the GST taxes due, but the amount of the GST taxes is based only on the gifted amount of the premiums rather than the higher death benefit! This enables a large amount of life insurance to be purchased tax-free and used tax-free by mulitple generations. This is just one example among a number of other opportunities that are available for you to take advantage of with Dynasty Trust planning.

Whether your estate is large or small, a Dynasty Trust can provide significant estate planning benefits. Do you want your grandchildren's inheritance, however modest or great, to be protected from abusive creditors, lawsuits, or future divorces? Do you want mulitple generations of your descendants to receive their inheritance federal estate tax-free? If you answer, "yes" to either of these questions, then you should seriously consider implementing a Dynasty Trust to protect your family.

CHAPTER TWELVE

CHARITABLE TRUSTS

A real win-win-win result is created by individuals or married couples who use one of the most powerful estate planning tools that exists—Charitable Trusts. There are two main kinds of Charitable Trusts—Charitable Remainder Trusts and Charitable Lead Trusts. The choice between these two options depends on the benefits you seek to obtain.

What are the benefits of creating a
Charitable Remainder Trust?

The benefits of creating a Charitable Remainder Trust can include the following:

- The Trustmakers win by: (a) gaining a lifetime income, while avoiding capital gains tax upon the sale of appreciated assets; (b) obtaining an immediate income tax deduction that can be carried forward for up to five years; (c) achieving a possible estate tax savings; and (d) creating a wonderful opportunity to accomplish their charitable dreams;

- The Trustmaker's chosen charities win by being the recipient of the Trustmaker's philanthropy; and

- Society wins because charities will promote social good and wisely use "social capital."

If any of these benefits sound intriguing, then the Charitable Remainder Trust might be just the answer to your estate planning needs.

What exactly is a Charitable Remainder Trust?

A Charitable Remainder Trust (CRT) is a special type of irrevocable trust in which the assets donated to it are shared between the Trustmakers and charitable beneficiaries. Typically, a CRT pays income to the Trustmakers for a number of years (or even the Trustmakers' entire lives), after which any remaining principal is paid to qualified charities.

What makes a CRT so beneficial?

Charitable Remainder Trusts offer you the ability to benefit from the sale of property that you might otherwise be hesitant to sell because of the capital gains taxes that would be due. CRTs are the result of special legislation that is intended to promote charitable giving by making it possible for you to gift highly appreciated assets (i.e., publicly traded stock, real estate, etc.) to a CRT capital gains tax-free. In turn, the trust provides an agreed upon annual income back to you, the Trustmaker. Additional benefits to you include an income tax charitable deduction as well as potential estate tax savings, because the assets are removed from your taxable estate once they are transferred to the CRT.

How does this compare with just selling the asset and buying income-producing assets?

A CRT is usually superior to an outright sale of assets. The capital gains tax-free sale of an asset to the CRT means that its entire value is working for you—not just the amount left over after the taxes are paid. Once the additional charitable income tax deduction and estate tax savings are factored in, the tax savings can be spectacular.

Can you provide examples of when a CRT should be considered?

A CRT should be considered an important planning option anytime the owner of an appreciated asset would like to sell it tax-free in order to obtain more income. The income provided by a CRT can be paid monthly, quarterly, or annually and, among other possibilities, used to increase your standard of living, provide for your retirement, assist elderly parents, fund a trust for a special needs child, or help your grandchildren go to college.

How can I use a CRT to help raise my standard of living?

Many of our clients have built up sizable estates through a lifetime of saving their hard earned money and living frugally. The newly available income provided from their CRT gives these clients the opportunity to remodel their home, buy a new car, go out more frequently, or take that long delayed vacation.

How can I use a CRT to help pay for my retirement?

If you are not able to make contributions to individual retirement accounts or other retirement plans, you can still use the tax-exempt status of a CRT to build the equivalent of a retirement plan for yourself.

For example, let's say that you are fifty-five years old and own stock for which you paid very little. It is now worth a substantial sum, but yields almost no income. If you sell the stock, you will owe capital gains taxes on the entire increase in value. This will leave less for you to reinvest for your retirement when you will need additional income. After careful thought and study, you decide to give the stock to a CRT. The trust can sell the stock without paying taxes on the gain. Since the entire value of the stock will be available to invest, you will receive more yearly income for the rest of your life than if you had sold the stock, paid the tax, and reinvested the balance. As an additional benefit, you will receive a charitable income tax deduction that can be used to offset some of your income.

How can I use a CRT to assist my elderly parents?

As our population ages, many working families are finding it necessary to save not only for their own retirement but also for the possibility that they will have to provide some financial assistance to their parents. Such assistance is not tax deductible and may result in gift tax consequences if it exceeds the permitted amount. A CRT offers a simple solution to this dilemma. You can transfer assets to a CRT that will provide a fixed income for life to an older relative instead of income for yourself. You will be entitled to a substantial charitable deduction for your gift to the trust and also be assured of proper management of the assets in the event you become unable to manage them yourself. At your parent's death, the trust ends and the assets will be distributed to your favorite charity—perhaps even in your parent's name.

How can I use a CRT to help my grandchildren go to college?

We are all faced with the rising cost of education. Every year those costs are increasing faster than inflation making it more difficult for parents to afford a quality education for their children. One solution to these escalating educational costs is for parents or grandparents to establish a CRT in which the income is used for a child's or grandchild's education.

If you give money directly to your children or grandchildren for their college expenses, the gift will not be tax deductible and it may even be subject to gift taxes. If you create a CRT, you will receive an immediate income tax deduction for the assets transferred to the CRT because when the trust ends, any remaining assets will be distributed for charitable purposes.

For example, assume you have a grandchild who will be starting college in a few years. Also assume that you own stock purchased many years ago that has increased substantially in value, but pays only small dividends.

You could sell the stock, pay the capital gains taxes, and then gift the remaining proceeds to your grandchild to pay for college. The gift, however, will not be tax deductible, it might be subject to gift taxation, and you will lose control over how your grandchild uses the money.

A wiser option might be to transfer the asset to a charitable trust designed to produce income for your grandchild's education. The CRT will then sell and invest the asset gift tax-free. Each year, according to your instructions, the CRT will pay a fixed amount only for your grandchild's education.

In this happier scenario, you will be entitled to a tax deduction for the transfer because the trust will last only a few years (up to the year of the budding scholar's anticipated college graduation) after which the remainder will be distributed for the charitable purposes you have selected.

A CRT sounds like a wonderful planning opportunity but are there any drawbacks?

Although a CRT is an excellent planning tool that can increase one's income, avoid unnecessary taxation, and achieve one's charitable planning dreams, one question that is frequently raised concerning them, usually by the Trustmaker's children, is: "What about our inheritance if everything in the CRT gets distributed as income or is left to a charity?"

It is not uncommon for the Trustmaker's children to view their parent's desire to create a CRT skeptically for the fear of being disinherited, or they may be suspicious that their parent is being unduly pressured by a charity into creating the CRT. Fortunately, these types of objections are easily overcome once the children learn that by establishing the CRT their parents can actually *increase* the children's inheritance and enable everyone (parents, charity, and children) to benefit.

The key to achieving this incredible *win win win* scenario lies in the fact that once the parents have established the CRT, they will be receiving a new stream of income. The parents can deal with the children's concerns about being disinherited by simply taking a fraction of that income and using it to purchase a new life insurance policy in an amount at least equal to the value of the asset transferred to the CRT.

Often the tax savings and additional income produced by the CRT enable the parents to purchase life insurance (also known as wealth replacement insurance) with a death benefit even greater than the value of the asset being transferred to the CRT. Even better, if the new life insurance policy is owned by an Irrevocable Life Insurance Trust (ILIT) created by the parents, the insurance proceeds will be outside the parent's estate and thus transferred to the children estate tax free. Most children are also pleased to learn that their inheritance will come in the form of a cash distribution from the ILIT instead of having to deal with selling a major asset after their parents die.

Now that I understand Charitable Remainder Trusts, how do they differ from Charitable Lead Trusts?

Both Charitable Remainder Trusts and Charitable Lead Trusts (CLT) result in gifts being made to a charity. They differ with respect to the timing of the gift. With a CRT, *the Trustmakers receive the trust's income* and the charity receives the assets remaining at the time the trust terminates, which is usually at the death of the Trustmaker or beneficiary. With a CLT *the charity receives the trust's income* and the Trustmaker (or the Trustmaker's selected beneficiary) receives the assets remaining at the time the trust terminates. Recipients of income and assets are reversed with a CLT compared to a CRT.

How can I use a CLT to benefit my family?

Assume that you desire to immediately help one of your favorite charities with the income produced by one of your assets (a rental apartment, for example) but you still want to ultimately keep the apartment itself in the family. At the same time you would also like to reduce your estate tax liability. A CRT will clearly not work in this situation. But a CLT might offer the ideal solution to accomplish these goals.

You could place your apartment into a CLT. A named charity will receive the rental income for the lifetime of the trust, after which time your children become the apartment's owners. Although your children will not receive the apartment building for a number of years, the value of your gift made to them, (for gift and estate tax purposes) must be calculated at the time the apartment is transferred to the CLT.

The value of an apartment received many years from now is not the same as the value of an apartment received today. No one would pay full price today for something they will receive only in the future. Accordingly, your children are entitled to *discount* the apartment's current fair market value in proportion to how long they have to wait to receive it.

It is this discounted value of the apartment, instead of its present fair market value, that is used to determine gift and estate taxes on your estate. The result can be a large tax savings to your children. In the meantime, rather than depreciating in value, the apartment building has actually continued to grow in value.

Your charity immediately benefits from the establishment of a CLT and your children will receive an asset that has appreciated in actual value yet has a substantially discounted value for estate tax purposes. Good things are possible for those who take the time to properly plan their estates! Your estate planning attorney will be able to help you determine whether a CRT or a CLT is an appropriate estate planning option for you.

CHAPTER THIRTEEN

LIMITED PARTNERSHIPS

Another powerful estate planning tool that can help a family plan for the future is the Limited Partnership. This tool can help family members diversify their investments and achieve significant savings of gift, estate, and income taxes. A Limited Partnership can also permit the older members of a family to retain control of assets while teaching younger members of the family how to best manage them and offer them significant asset protection.

What exactly is a Limited Partnership?

A Limited Partnership is a business entity established under state law. Ownership of the partnership is broken into two classes of partners—general and limited. The distinction between a general partner and a limited partner is important because it determines whether you will have a say in the partnership's management or whether you receive liability protection from the partnership's activities. Limited Partnerships are frequently used by family members or business associates to facilitate transfers of assets to others, often at a discounted value that permits significant tax savings.

What are the liability protections provided by a Limited Partnership?

An important aspect of limited partnerships is that only general partners, not limited partners, have any say in the management of the partnership. This means that the general partners (usually the parents or older generation) entirely control it and are the only ones personally liable for the partnership's business dealings.

Since the limited partners have no say in the partnership's control or management, normally they are not personally liable for partnership liabilities and risk only their investment in the partnership. A Limited Partnership offers important asset protection planning opportunities for those seeking to protect their personal assets.

What are the tax benefits provided by a Limited Partnership?

A Limited Partnership provides significant opportunities to reduce your estate taxes. In fact, many partnerships are created principally because the partners receive significant accounting discounts in the value of property transferred to the partnership. The greater the discounted value of the property transferred to the partnership, the lower its taxable value for gift and estate tax purposes.

The ability to discount an asset's value when transferred to a Limited Partnership is a result of how assets are valued on the free market. The Internal Revenue Service and Tax Courts recognize that the fair market value of an asset over which you possess total control is greater than the fair market value of an asset over which you possess little control. No one would pay the same price for a business controlled by others (even family members), as they would pay for a business they could run as they pleased.

A Limited Partnership is an attractive estate planning tool because, due to the limited partner's lack of control over the management of partnership assets, a legitimate discount in the asset's free market value will be available for the partnership interest.

Generally speaking, the less control a limited partner has in the partnership, the greater the valuation discount given. In order to obtain the maximum discount, many partnership agreements intentionally contain many restrictions on the rights of limited partners to be involved in partnership decisions, to withdraw from the partnership, and even on their right to sell their partnership interests. Such partnership restrictions must not be more severe than those permitted by state law or they will be disregarded for the calculation of any discount.

Limited Partnerships can also be coupled with gifting strategies to help you reduce estate taxes. To accomplish this, you would first create a Limited Partnership and transfer assets (such as a family business) to it. Then over a period of years you would slowly transfer partnership interests to your children who are made limited partners. The value of the partnership interests transferred is intentionally kept below the annual gift tax exemption amount so as to avoid any gift tax liability. When done correctly, this strategy can transfer a significant part of the estate to the children gift and estate tax-free while keeping the parents in total control.

A Limited Partnership can also be used by families to provide income tax savings to family members. Subject to certain restrictions, the members of a Limited Partnership can allocate income and deductions among the general and limited partners in any agreed upon way. This ability to allocate income to individual partners permits a family to distribute partnership income to lower tax bracket members.

What factors need to be considered before establishing a Limited Partnership?

Before organizing a Limited Partnership, you should seek the advice of your estate planning attorney concerning a multitude of issues. Those issues include selection of the general partner and deciding who will be responsible for the partnership's day-to-day management.

Also, since a general partner has unlimited liability for partnership liabilities and losses, the desires of the partners concerning liability for the partnership's business transactions and their desires regarding the protection of their personal assets from partnership liabilities must be examined. Additionally, the level of trust that the partners have in each other must be considered because the actions of one general partner can legally bind the others.

Taxation of business entity issues must also be examined. Limited partnerships are a *flow-through entity*. This means that the partnership's income and deductions are reported on each partner's individual tax return. The partnership itself pays no federal income tax, a significant benefit over corporations, which normally are taxed at the corporate level.

Other tax ramifications should also be considered. Organizing exclusively as a Limited Partnership may foreclose some tax planning opportunities, particularly in the area of employee benefits. A careful planner will make you aware that a corporation or limited liability company (LLC) can serve as a general partner.

This option may be appropriate because a corporation or LLC can provide employee benefits and other planning opportunities not available to partnerships. If a corporation or LLC is chosen to act as the general partner, it is possible to have the corporate or LLC general partner elect "S Corporation" tax status. This permits the continuation of flow-through taxation at the individual level.

How do I know if a Limited Partnership is right for me?

A Limited Partnership is an excellent tool that empowers you to maintain control over assets while at the same time offering you the flexibility needed to devise and implement a sound estate planning strategy that can deal simultaneously with a multitude of business and family issues. These issues require an analysis of your assets, your business succession desires, how control over the partnership is to be allocated between general and limited partners, the asset protection consequences, and the estate, gift, and income tax ramifications.

Of course, by itself a Limited Partnership is not a complete estate plan. It works best in conjunction with your Revocable Living Trust and other planning documents to make sure that your estate planning desires are completely fulfilled. It is important to discuss these serious issues in depth with your estate planning attorney before deciding whether a Limited Partnership is an appropriate tool in your estate plan. Although we live in a time when many less than scrupulous individuals are trying to sell fill-in-the-blank partnership forms, only a qualified estate planning attorney will be able to help you sort out your options and tailor a plan that will best protect your family.

CHAPTER FOURTEEN

ASSET PROTECTION

Building a successful estate, although it takes a lifetime of hard work, is only half of the battle. Just as big a challenge, if not more so, is safeguarding your wealth from a host of threats that seek to rob you of your hard-earned financial security. No one is immune. Taxes, lawsuits, creditor actions, even divorces can shake the foundations of the most financially secure. In fact, anyone who has managed to accumulate assets, whether a home, business, rental property, investments, or other valuable property, can be subject to so-called "predator" actions. The more wealth you own, the more enticing a target you become to those eager to deprive you and your family of the fruits of your life's work.

Although we all share the danger of being targeted by such predators, the risk is realistically greater for some than for others. Those most often targeted by lawsuits and creditor actions are usually involved in high-risk professions. These include doctors, lawyers, accountants, business managers, financial advisors, engineers, architects, and other professional advisors. But also clearly in predators' sights are business owners, employers, landlords, and contractors, among others. Having substantial financial resources may be all it takes to put you on the wrong end of a lawsuit.

If such predators pose a threat to your financial security, it would be wise for you to explore the legal options that exist for you to protect your assets for yourself and your family. Such legal options to protect your estate fall under the category of "asset protection" planning.

What is asset protection planning?

Put simply, asset protection planning is the process of removing your property from your individual ownership and placing it beyond the reach of potential claimants and creditors. The process involves changing legal ownership of your property from your individual name to a protective entity, such as a limited partnership or trust.

If that sounds like a terrible idea, hold on. A properly designed limited partnership or trust can give you all the benefits of ownership, such as control over an asset's disposition and the right to its income. The difference is that since you no longer legally own the asset, it cannot be seized to satisfy a judgment against you. It is the savvy planner who realizes that in today's world legal control over an asset is often more beneficial than directly owning it.

What asset protection does a Limited Partnership provide?

As stated in the preceding chapter, Limited Partnerships offer significant asset protection opportunities. Limited partnerships provide such asset protection because of the way the laws that govern partnerships treat partners and partnership assets. As you will recall, limited partnerships have two kinds of partners, each with dramatically different roles and responsibilities. General partners manage the partnership, and thus have full responsibility and control.

Limited partners, on the other hand, have little, if any, input into the running of the partnership; therefore, they are not held responsible for its management or any liability it might create. No one would want to become a limited partner without this protection. The law is designed to encourage the creation of partnerships and the economic benefits they produce for society.

The second important feature of limited partnerships is that assets titled in the name of the partnership are deemed the property of the partnership itself, not that of the individual partners. The legal importance of this arrangement is that partnership assets are shielded from creditor claims against the individual partners. In other words, a creditor cannot force the sale of assets owned by the partnership to satisfy a judgment against one of its members. Instead, such creditors are entitled to attach only the member's individually owned assets and to receive any distributions made by the partnership to that member.

To achieve asset protection with a Limited Partnership, you would transfer individual assets (real estate, business interests, investments, artwork, etc.) out of your personal name and into the name of the Limited Partnership. A common arrangement would be for you to become a one percent general partner, giving you the right to fully control and manage property just as before. You would also become a ninety-nine percent limited partner, entitling you to receive income from the partnership, but shielding your limited partnership assets from creditor claims. For the greatest asset protection, most individuals who use Limited Partnerships transfer part of their limited partnership shares to others, usually family members. This shows that the partnership has legitimate business purposes other than just defeating creditor claims and makes them more likely to survive a court challenge. Because Limited Partnerships can provide significant tax advantages, as well as asset protection, it is often an ideal strategy to use when an individual wants to pass wealth, especially a business, to other family members.

Sometimes a Limited Partnership alone isn't enough protection against possible lawsuits or creditor actions. That's when an Offshore Trust becomes an important tool in the asset protection toolkit.

What is an Offshore Trust?

An Offshore Trust is simply a trust created outside of the legal jurisdiction of the United States. These Offshore Trusts are effective in protecting assets simply because the laws of the nations in which they are drafted provide better creditor protection than the protections provided in the United States of America.

Why do Offshore Trusts provide better asset protection?

In the United States, generally no asset protection exists for assets that you place in a trust created to benefit yourself and for which you are the trustee. In such cases, the trust's assets can be seized by your creditors just as if they were owned in your own name.

However, a handful of other nations—such as the Isle of Man, the Cook Islands, and Belize, to name a few—offer Trustmakers greater asset protection. These nations allow you to be the Trustmaker, Trustee, and the Trust Beneficiary and still protect the trust's assets from creditors.

Furthermore, these countries will not honor a United States Court's judgment or lien against trust assets in their jurisdiction. Before a creditor can seize trust assets, these nations require that a trial be held on their soil. The creditor must pay the often exorbitant fees associated with litigating a case in a foreign country. The cost of bringing witnesses and other legal evidence to a foreign court can prove prohibitive, as can the legal fees of a local attorney. Legal fees alone can prove a costly and insurmountable burden to bringing a lawsuit, as the trust-favorable nations do not allow for contingency fee lawsuits. Instead, they require that the plaintiff's attorney be paid without regard to the outcome of the action.

If this were not enough in the way of asset protection, these nations also demand that the plaintiff meet the burden of proof required in United States criminal courts. A creditor plaintiff must prove its case "beyond a reasonable doubt," not the much more lax "preponderance of evidence" standard used in the United States.

Finally, the countries most favorable to Offshore Trusts greatly limit the amount of time allowed to a plaintiff to bring legal action. In the United States, plaintiffs often have many years to file a lawsuit but in these offshore nations, plaintiffs have only a year or two to bring suit, depending on the circumstances. So for those desiring greater asset protection, Offshore Trusts can provide immeasurable peace of mind.

How do you establish an Offshore Trust?

To obtain the legal protections offered by Offshore Trusts, typically you would have your attorney create both a limited partnership and a trust in the desired offshore nation. You would then transfer your ninety-nine percent limited partnership shares to the Offshore Trust and retain the one-percent general partner share. Doing this would afford you the greatest possible degree of protection for your wealth, while preserving complete control over the assets themselves.

Fortunately, Offshore Trust laws do not require that the assets literally be removed from U.S. soil nor do they require that the Trustmaker relocate to a foreign country. As long as the ownership of the assets and the jurisdiction governing the trust reside in a trust-favorable nation, the Trustmaker receives full asset protection.

What factors need to be considered before establishing an Offshore Trust?

The reality is that asset protection planning is more costly to implement than other estate plans. In addition, you'll spend more each year to maintain it but keep in mind the savings it can also generate. You may be able to reduce considerably the malpractice or business liability insurance premiums you now pay once most of your assets are protected offshore. Furthermore, you can save the enormous cost of defending yourself in a lawsuit, or worse, losing it all in court. With proper asset protection in place, you may never have to experience either. The peace of mind alone afforded by this planning option is often well worth the modest investment.

If an Offshore Trust makes sense to you, the time to implement it is now before it is too late and a legal crisis is already upon you. If you wait until action against you is "pending, threatened, or expected," the measures you take to remove wealth from your estate will be deemed a fraudulent conveyance and invalidated by a court of law.

Moreover, don't think that an Offshore Trust will lessen your tax liability. If you remove assets offshore, you are required to notify the IRS and pay U.S. taxes on trust earnings.

One final note is also in order. In an attempt to capture some of the Offshore Trust business, a few states recently enacted laws which promise to provide trusts created under their jurisdiction with some of the same protections offered by trusts created in foreign jurisdictions. While it's possible that these trusts may work for those who live, work, and own all their assets in one of these states, those in other states may be exposed to creditor action just as before because each state's courts are required to give "full faith and credit" to the judgments of other states' courts. A judgment against you in one state would be honored by the other states, even if the trust you've created seemed to promise you complete protection.

If you think that asset protection may be for you, sit down immediately with your trusted estate planning attorney. It is your attorney who can evaluate your individual situation and determine the most effective strategy to help you meet your asset protection goals.

CHAPTER FIFTEEN

FEDERAL ESTATE AND GIFT TAXES

Despite its promises to "simplify" the tax code, Congress' never ending changes to our nation's estate and gift tax code have made it too complicated for most people to understand. Nonetheless, a review of its basic details is essential to understanding how to protect your estate.

What are federal estate and gift taxes?

Federal estate and gift taxes are known as transfer taxes. Simply put, they are taxes on your right to give money or property to others. The gift tax is a tax on your right to give money away while you are alive. The estate tax is a tax on your right to leave your property to others at your death.

Why should I be concerned about these taxes?

In effect, federal estate and gift taxes constitute a double tax on your assets. Not only are your assets taxed when first earned, but then your lifetime savings are taxed a second time when you try to pass them to your children. Without proper planning, these taxes can take up to fifty percent of your life savings. That should be of concern to all of us.

Is there a way to avoid these taxes?

Fortunately, federal estate and gift taxes are mostly avoidable for those who take the time and effort to plan their estates. Unfortunately, most people do not plan their estates and therefore never learn if they have a taxable estate. They consequently risk the danger of having to pay otherwise unnecessary taxes.

How do I know if I have a taxable estate?

Whether or not you have a taxable estate depends initially on how much property you own at the time of your death. This is therefore an individual issue. The size of your taxable estate is calculated by first adding up the current fair market value of everything that you own (your assets) and then subtracting your debts and mortgages. Your assets include your home and any other real estate, business holdings, checking and savings accounts, certificates of deposit, stocks, mutual funds, bonds, individual retirement accounts, 401(k) plans, pensions and any personal property you own.

Most people do not realize that, in addition to all of the above assets, the *death benefits* from any life insurance policies that you own are also included in calculating the size of your taxable estate. Any taxable gifts made during your entire life will also be added because federal tax law is written to make sure you do not avoid estate taxes at your death by giving everything away while you are still alive.

What is the applicable exclusion amount?

Rather than taxing all estates, no matter how small, Congress has determined that everyone is entitled at death to transfer to others a given amount of property estate tax-free. This set amount of property that can be transferred tax-free is called the "applicable exclusion amount". The actual amount of the exclusion is changed rather frequently by Congress. It is also reduced by the value of any taxable gifts made during the taxpayer's lifetime.

How are gift taxes calculated?

Congress has decided that gifts made during your lifetime that exceed the annual gift tax exemption will be subject to gift taxes. Gifts that are below the annual exemption are gift tax-free. The annual exemption is indexed for inflation, so it is necessary to check with your estate planning attorney for the current annual exemption amount.

In addition to the annual gift tax exclusion, everyone also has a lifetime exclusion. If you make a gift that exceeds the annual exclusion, you are required to file a gift tax report with the IRS, which keeps track of your gifts. At your death, all taxable gifts made during your lifetime are added together to determine the total amount of taxable gifts made. The amount of all lifetime taxable gifts is then subtracted from your applicable exclusion. The amount of applicable exclusion you have left determines how much property your estate can pass on estate tax-free at the time of your death.

Once you have calculated the federal applicable exclusion that your estate is entitled to pass on tax-free, you can check the exclusion amount against the size of your taxable estate. This will reveal how much estate tax your estate will have to pay. A qualified estate planning attorney can help you calculate the current exemption amount that your estate is entitled to and determine if your estate will be liable for estate taxes.

What happens if I have a taxable estate?

Federal estate taxes are due and must be paid no later than nine months after the date of death to avoid penalties and interest. Additionally, the tax must be paid in cash. If your estate is going to be subject to the estate tax, you need to plan to provide this needed cash through assets that are readily and easily converted to cash.

This need to raise cash quickly is frequently the reason estates are forced to rapidly sell assets, including businesses, at fire sale prices; therefore, one significant goal of your estate plan should be to minimize or eliminate the estate tax.

Even if your estate is liable for estate taxes, there is still some good news. Usually these taxes can be paid in installments over a period of many years and in some circumstances, the government allows very favorable interest rates during the payment period. If taxes are due, your estate planning attorney will be able to help you select the best way to pay them.

How can I minimize or eliminate estate taxes?

Although federal estate taxation is poised to pounce on the unwary, there are fortunately both exceptions to the tax and strategies to legitimately plan around it. For example, a major exception to the estate tax exists for married couples. Under the federal tax code, all amounts left to a spouse are exempt from estate taxation. This exemption for spousal transfers is known as the "unlimited marital deduction". The unlimited marital deduction may sound like an easy way for a couple to avoid estate taxes, but it only works if you have a spouse who survives you.

The government is not concerned about taxing the estate of the first spouse to die if it is all left to the surviving spouse. The IRS knows it will be able to collect the taxes on the combined estate when the spouse dies. The larger the survivor's estate, the larger the tax bill. Estates that would otherwise have been below the applicable exclusion (and thus tax-free if taxed separately), become taxable once they are combined and are artificially pushed into higher tax brackets.

As you can see, it would be best from a tax planning perspective if a couple's estates were taxed separately. In order for this to occur, we need to devise a plan that is better than the old way of just leaving everything at our deaths directly to the surviving spouse. In addition, our new plan must still make sure the surviving spouse is properly cared for and kept in control of the estate after the first spouse dies. If only there were a way to provide for the surviving spouse and still enable the estates to be taxed separately. Fortunately, there is! It starts by wisely using the applicable exclusion of *both* spouses.

One way to view the applicable exclusion is to think of it as a tax-free "coupon" that the government gives each of us. This is a most valuable coupon because it can be redeemed to pay the huge tax bill that would otherwise be imposed on our estates. Since each of us is given an exclusion coupon, a married couple has two such coupons.

The problem is that most of us just toss away the coupon of the first spouse to die. Instead of using the decedent's exclusion coupon to render tax-free some or all of the decedent's estate, we just pass everything to the surviving spouse and let our estates be combined. The result is that estate taxes are deferred because of the unlimited marital deduction, but not avoided.

A much better planning strategy for the family is to use both coupons. This strategy starts with the couple creating a "family trust" that is funded, up to the estate tax exclusion amount, with the property of the first spouse to die. Such family trusts are established for the benefit of the surviving spouse and children and can be used for practically anything that maintains their lifestyle.

The decedent spouse's exclusion coupon is then used to offset any taxes that would otherwise be due. This renders everything in the family trust estate tax free while still enabling it to be used for the surviving family.

The family's remaining assets are placed in a "marital trust" that can be completely under the control of the surviving spouse for the spouse's enjoyment and benefit. When the second spouse dies, his or her remaining exclusion coupon is used to render the assets in the marital trust tax-free up to the exclusion amount. The end result is that the surviving spouse stays in control of the entire estate while maximizing the family's tax-planning opportunities.

It is important to realize, however, that the above tax-planning strategy must be implemented while both spouses are still alive. When one dies it is too late; thus, it is best to be proactive and immediately take advantage of the benefits that the law provides by planning your estate now.

What if the federal estate tax law changes?

Congress is constantly tinkering with the exemption amount and what the law is today may, and probably will, change tomorrow. A good estate plan will be solid enough to avoid the taxes that would be imposed if you died today while still remaining flexible enough to be amended to keep up with changes in the law. Estate planning should not be viewed as a one-time affair. Instead, a good estate plan should be periodically reviewed to keep it current with changes in the family as well as changes in the law.

Regardless of what happens in the future, good planning is always based on the situation that exists today with an eye to tomorrow. The reality is that if your estate is taxable today, and you or your spouse die today, you will have lost the significant tax avoidance opportunities to which your family is entitled.

Speculation that the estate tax will be eliminated is not a valid reason to forego implementing your estate plan. Speculation concerning the future should never be a substitute for planning that is needed today. Furthermore, even if the federal estate tax is fully revoked, history teaches us that Congress has, and probably will, re-enact it again in a few years.

The estate tax, like the phoenix, continues to be resurrected. In fact, the twentieth century saw the estate tax imposed and repealed several times.

Regardless of what happens with the federal estate tax, there are separate but equally important issues that any sound estate plan needs to consider: Probate avoidance, asset protection, disability planning, and a host of other benefits already mentioned in this book are not tax related but can still provide great benefits to you and your family. In addition, each state also has the authority to impose estate taxes. The issue of state estate taxation is addressed in the next chapter.

CHAPTER SIXTEEN

STATE ESTATE TAXES

In addition to federal estate taxes, most of us also face the dreaded prospect of having to pay state estate taxes. Even if you live in a state that does not impose an estate tax, you may have assets located in a state that does have an estate tax.

Historically, instead of imposing their own completely separate estate tax, most state governments opted to share in the estate taxes collected by the federal government. The government referred to this method of sharing with the states as a "pickup tax". In reality, it was a kick-back to the states of a portion of the tax the federal government collected.

Federal law eliminated the pickup tax which resulted in a drastic cut in the amount of revenue the states received from estate tax. Many states, having become accustomed to receiving this extra money each year from the federal government, have subsequently established their own "state death tax" laws to enable them to continue to collect the tax.

While some states have abolished state estate taxes, others

continue to impose the tax upon land and property you own at death. In many instances state taxes may take a small but annoying bite out of your estate. But in some states, death taxes can be steep.

How will these state taxes affect me?

First, the state imposed taxes will be assessed regardless of what Congress does on the federal level. Therefore, if you desire to pass your estate without losing a substantial amount in estate taxes, you need to plan to avoid state estate taxes in addition to any federal estate tax.

If you expect to leave an estate worth less than the exempt level established by both the federal and state governments, you may not need to worry about death taxes. However, each state sets its own exemption amount, which is subject to change at any time. If you have an estate larger than the exempt amount, or if you are planning to leave your property to your spouse, who may then have an estate exceeding the exempt level, you may wish to learn more about how to reduce estate taxes to the lowest possible amount.

Second, the new state inheritance taxes have made estate planning much more challenging. Formerly, estate planning was needed to avoid just the federal estate tax, but now estate planning must simultaneously take both taxes into consideration. This is not a simple task since the two tax codes can follow different rules. Planning to avoid one tax could trigger the other. For example, if your estate plan is designed to avoid the maximum possible amount of federal estate taxes, it might trigger a state estate tax at the death of the first spouse in those states where the state exemption is lower than the federal exemption. Conversely, if your plan is designed to completely avoid state estate taxes, it could sacrifice your ability to avoid federal estate taxes.

The decision as to which of these two taxes to avoid is an individual one that needs to take into account your family's planning goals, as well as the tax consequences of planning to avoid one tax versus the other. You must make a well-informed decision that best protects your family. A qualified estate planning attorney will be needed to help you sort through these complex issues and help you evaluate whether a state death tax will apply to your situation.

CHAPTER SEVENTEEN

TRUST ADMINISTRATION

The administration of most estates is strewn with the confusion, loss of control, delay, and expense of probate court proceedings due to the lack of, or poor, estate planning. At the worst possible time the family is forced to face these legal hurdles. A well-designed living trust centered plan, however, will help ease the burden for your loved ones. It does this by helping you to easily transfer your assets to those you want to receive them.

When a Trustmaker dies, the surviving family should contact the estate planning attorney who drafted the trust as soon as possible. That attorney will be in the best position to readily understand the planning that was done and advise the family about the steps needed to administer the estate.

The ideal time is within the first few days following the Trustmaker's death. There are two reasons to follow this suggestion. First, your estate planning attorney will want to schedule an initial meeting with the trustees and beneficiaries. It is a good idea, if possible, to schedule this meeting while loved ones are still in town for memorial services.

A second reason to immediately schedule a meeting is to protect the planning that was done. Those who plan their estates with a living trust usually take great care and provide detailed instructions for how they want their estates to be administered. It is therefore *extremely important* that family members do not sell, transfer, or mix trust assets without first receiving legal counsel. Without proper administration, tax planning strategies can be jeopardized or lost and the Trustmaker's desires unintentionally thwarted. The family should never make financial decisions concerning trust property without first consulting with an attorney.

What happens at the initial administration meeting?

At the initial administration meeting your attorney will discuss a number of issues with your loved ones. The first order of business is ensuring an ongoing income for your spouse and any dependent children. A well-crafted trust document will always have arrangements for such immediate needs. Family members will be especially relieved to avoid the expense and stress of probate court proceedings which can be time consuming and greatly delay access to the estate's assets. In contrast, a trust-based plan will offer your loved ones immediate access to your funds free of court interference.

What else needs to be addressed after my spouse and children are taken care of?

After reassuring a surviving spouse and children that they are taken care of, the attorney will review the steps that need to be taken to properly administer the estate. Even with a trust, a certain amount of work is always needed to properly wrap up the estate. Your attorney will discuss the following questions with your family members:

- Who are the successor trustees? What are their duties and what instructions do they need to carry out?

- How will the successor trustees gain access to your financial information and assets to implement your estate plan?

- How are the estate's assets valued?

- How are life insurance claims submitted?

- How are retirement plan benefits claimed and what decisions need to be made concerning options to roll them into a surviving spouse's name or otherwise minimize distributions?

- Does the estate owe any debts and how will they get paid?

- What are the likely administrative expenses and how will they get paid?

- How will income tax returns get prepared and filed for the final year of life?

- How will the estate's income tax returns get prepared and filed?

- How will any necessary gift or estate tax returns be prepared and filed?

- How will assets be distributed to the beneficiaries?

Your accountant, financial advisor, and insurance agent will help with some of these tasks. Your attorney will work with a team of these professionals to set timetables, track deadlines, and coordinate the process for your loved ones.

How are tax issues handled?

One of the purposes of a properly prepared and funded living trust is to minimize taxes; however, even with a trust some taxes may be due. After the death of a Trustmaker, the estate planning team of professionals will work together to see that tax returns are prepared and arrangements are made to pay proper taxes on personal, trust, and estate income. Additionally, your attorney will work to fairly allocate income taxes to your beneficiaries on their inheritance, and try to minimize the tax consequences to your estate.

One of the estate planning tools often used to minimize taxes is called a *disclaimer*. A disclaimer is the legal right of a beneficiary or spouse to refuse any distribution from a trust. The use of a disclaimer can often be an effective tool used by an attorney to redirect funds from an individual to your trust. This can benefit the family by minimizing taxes and maximizing the long-term benefits of the trust, such as asset protection. Accordingly, your estate planning attorney will be alert for opportunities to take advantage of a disclaimer strategy. Unless the family's legal right to disclaim property into the trust is properly used, the disclaimer right will be lost. That is why it is so vital that your loved ones not sell or transfer assets from your trust without first receiving proper legal advice.

How long does a trust administration take?

One of the purposes of a properly drafted and funded trust is to prevent the need for a probate proceeding so that your loved ones can return to their everyday lives as soon as possible. Even so, the length of time it will take to properly administer your trust will vary depending on several factors. These factors include the size of the estate, whether the trust was fully funded, the type of assets that exist, and any requirement to pay taxes, but it will be your family, and not the courts, who will be able to settle the estate on their terms and at a time of their choosing. Most trust administrations will take a fraction of the time needed to probate an estate.

How do the costs of administrating a trust compare with probating a will?

The costs of administering a trust include attorney and accountant fees, court costs and appraisers' fees when needed. Your estate planning attorney will work with your family to review the instructions given in your estate plan, identify your wishes, and advise and coordinate with the estate planning team on all legal issues including its administration. This involves the collection and distribution of trust assets, the exercise of legal disclaimer rights, the preparation and filing of tax returns, the handling of any guardianship issues, the valuation of assets, the collection of life insurance proceeds, the handling of retirement benefits, the payment of debts and administrative expenses, and the transfer of assets to your beneficiaries or the trusts established for them. While every case is unique, attorney fees for trust administration services typically average one and one half percent or less of estate assets. Fees are usually based on the estate's complexity and whether or not your trust was fully funded during your lifetime.

This compares very favorably with the cost of probating a will, which often consumes 3% to 8% of the total estate. Additionally, the estate taxes on your assets, if you rely on a simple will instead of a trust, could cost your family hundreds of thousands of dollars of unnecessary estate taxes. Although wills generally cost less than trusts to initially prepare, a comparative analysis of the two shows that a trust-based plan will ultimately cost far less while also simplifying the settlement process for your loved ones.

The loss of a loved one is difficult enough without the added burden of having to administer an estate that is overly cumbersome and costly. Your estate planning attorney will work with your loved ones to avoid court proceedings, taxes, and other legal pitfalls. A trust-centered estate plan and administration will give you the peace of mind of knowing that, following your death, your loved ones' financial needs will be properly taken care of and their lives disrupted as little as possible.

CHAPTER EIGHTEEN

HOW TO SELECT AN ESTATE PLANNING ATTORNEY

Finding the right attorney to plan your estate can be a significant challenge. For many people, choosing an attorney to plan their estate is the first contact they have had with an attorney. It can be a daunting task for them to decide what qualities they should look for in an estate planning attorney.

Others simply accept on faith that any attorney is competent to plan their estate. Such confidence is frequently misplaced because many attorneys have little training or actual experience in this complex area of law.

Still others yield to the temptation to shop for price rather than quality in legal services. When it comes to obtaining quality estate planning services, as with most other areas in life, you get what you pay for and your selection should be made with care and based on more than cost.

How should I go about selecting a qualified estate planning attorney?

Selecting a qualified attorney should not be a matter of luck or happenstance. We offer the following tips to provide you with the information needed to meaningfully interview and select an estate planning attorney who has the experience and training to do an excellent job for you.

- Interview only attorneys whose practices are dedicated to planning estates. Other attorneys simply don't have the knowledge or experience to plan your estate properly. Planning an estate is the equivalent of legal heart surgery. You would not go to a family doctor for heart surgery. Do not go to a general practitioner for estate planning.

- Ask if the attorney will help you avoid the additional costs, delays, loss of privacy, and other problems of probate. Many so-called "Estate Planning Attorneys" actually earn their living by probating estates at the surviving family's expense. Also, since the probate court process will make a public record of all of your private affairs, an attorney who designs an estate plan for you that requires your estate to be probated is essentially depriving your family of the privacy it needs and deserves.

- Hire only an attorney that you like and trust. After qualifications and experience, nothing is more important in planning your estate than having a relationship with your attorney that is built on friendship and mutual trust.

- Determine the law office's procedure for handling client requests for information and performing legal work before you hire it. You have the right to demand excellent legal service from your attorney. Anything less is not acceptable.

- Find out if the attorney will return your phone calls quickly. An attorney's office that is slow in responding to your calls will probably be slow in everything. Find someone else.

- Ask if the attorney will quote you a fixed fee for designing and implementing your estate plan. This will save you the surprise of and probable anger at receiving an unexpectedly large legal bill.

- Inquire whether the attorney offers an annual review of your estate plan. Those that do are the most dedicated to seeing that your estate plan will be kept up-to-date.

- Determine whether the attorney can prepare your estate planning documents within a month's time. This is a realistic timeframe for an attorney who knows the law and provides efficient services.

- Interview only attorneys who understand and believe in the benefits of trust-centered planning as demonstrated by the use of trusts for their own personal planning. Do not deal with attorneys who fail to personally believe in the services they provide to others.

- Choose only an estate planning attorney who offers comprehensive estate planning services. The goal of a complete estate plan is to provide you with the peace of mind that comes from knowing your legacy will be transferred exactly according to your stated desires. Your plan will not succeed as expected unless your living trust is supplemented with several additional legal documents. These include financial powers of attorney, health care directives, guardianship nominations, and property agreements, to name just a few. An attorney that provides quality services will also provide detailed instructions on how to fund and maintain your trust. Ask the attorney for a detailed list of the services offered and the documents typically provided.

- Be sure you can read and understand your estate planning documents. The days of a secret legal language are long past. There is simply no way to be assured that your estate planning documents fulfill your desires unless you can understand them. Consider asking to see a sample of the documents typically provided.

- See if your estate planning documents will be neatly assembled in an estate planning portfolio. Such a portfolio will keep the documents readily available so you and your family can easily find them whenever desired and ensure they are not difficult to find in emergencies.

- It is critical that the attorney remain current with changes to estate planning laws that affect your estate. Congress, state legislatures, Tax Courts, and the IRS issue new laws, regulations, and decisions on a continuous basis that affect your planning. Ask the attorney for the process used to remain on the cutting edge of the law. Dedicated estate planning attorneys will be members of professional organizations which meet regularly to share information, review and study estate planning issues.

We believe that only an attorney who possesses these characteristics and offers these services will provide you with the quality estate planning services you and your loved ones need and deserve.

Estate planning involves reviewing and analyzing your desires and finances *today* to insure that you and your family are prepared for tomorrow. It requires that you have a team of qualified professionals that will work together to make sure you receive an integrated estate plan of the highest quality. The captain of that team should be a qualified estate planning attorney who has the training and experience to turn your estate planning desires into reality. You deserve the best estate planning services possible and we, the authors of this book, are committed to providing you with nothing less.